God's Got a Habit :

God's Unconditional Love

THINKING MORE
LIKE GOD IN 30 DAYS
A WOMEN'S DEVOTIONAL

BY TAMARA M. KNIGHT

God's Got a Habit: God's Unconditional Love

By Tamara M. Knight

The Church Online, LLC
1000 Ardmore Blvd.
Pittsburgh, PA 15221

International Standard Book Number:
978-1-940786-94-0

Published by The Church Online, LLC

CONTENTS

FOREWARD

How long does it take to develop a habit? 21, 30 or 60 days? Well, it depends on how committed you are to the habit. If it's eating right Or exercise it may take as long as 60 days, including falling off the wagon once or twice.

But what about daily devotions? Seems like that should be easier, but it all depends.

It's got to be convenient, easy to put your hands on, that's the first step.

We're all busy, it has to be easy to digest, that's step two.

Relevance, that's step three. If I can't apply to every day life, I can't use it.

And lastly, if it's going to become my habit, it has to make a difference. For me, and the women I know, we are already juggling work, kids, grands, husbands, and on and on.

If I give you 30 days to develop a habit I want results. But results in this case are complicated. You can't track them on the scale, Or your bank account or scratching things off your to do list. But you will know when you begin to feel at peace at the beginning or the end of each day. When your conversations with God start to feel easier, and the idea of checking in with him everyday becomes second nature.

I started reading this daily devotional during the 2020 pandemic. I had adapted to my new stay at home life. I liked the slower pace. I didn't have to say no to requests for appearances or speaking engagements. The pandemic did that for me. I finally had time to focus on me , my growth and my relationship with God. I didn't know exactly what empty space I needed to fill in my life but by Day 8, "The word is the key to survival", I knew I found not just the space, but what would it would take to fill it.

I needed to take a few minutes everyday just for me and God; but in a way that made me feel really connected... like I didn't want to miss it. Something that had to happen everyday.

That's when I knew exactly how long it took to develop a habit.

30 Days.

Lynne Hayes Freeland
KDKA-TV | CBS Pittsburgh

WEEK 1:
First of All

GOD IS ABLE!

If we are thrown into the blazing furnace, the God we serve is able to deliver us from it, and he will deliver us from Your Majesty's hand. —*Daniel 3:17*

When I was about five years of age, my parents took us to our family picnic at a local amusement park. I was deathly afraid of a popular ride in the children's section at the time. My mom and auntie put my cousin and me on the ride as my father talked to friends. Since it was harmless, my mom hoped I'd conquer my fear of water as I rode down a tiny river in a little boat that passed under a watermill. Easy, right? Uh, NO! I was terrified of the idea! Still, I agreed to get into the tiny vessel, and I did so with the utmost caution and tears streaming down my face.

As our boat moved toward the watermill, I looked behind us, and my parents disappeared further and further into the distance. As the sound of the water falling from the watermill grew louder and louder, and the roaring of the mill shook the boat, my fear grew stronger and my crying more intense. I couldn't believe my parents were going to let my cousin and me drown. We weren't afraid; it was just me. My cousin was fine. I thought that because she was just a little younger, she didn't realize we were going to die soon. So, I took matters into my own hands. I looked past my mom, down to my dad, and yelled, "Daddy, please help me!" My dad turned around, took one look at my face, and jumped into the water. He caught up with us and snatched me out of the boat right before it went under the mill.

My cousin survived the ride and the effects of my traumatizing behavior like a trouper that day. Turns out she knew all along that we could just stand up to survive if, against all odds, we happened to fall out the boat. Despite the excitement, I learned an additional lesson that day. I found that my dad was exactly who I thought he was: Superman. The moment I went into distress, I knew I had to get my dad's attention. Why? Simply because my dad was able to keep me from harm. Dad was going to rescue me no matter what. I didn't know if he was going to grab me out the boat, stop the mill, or tell me not to worry and coach me through it. The point was, Daddy could do whatever it took to aid me.

This is what the three Hebrew boys concluded prior to being thrown into the fiery furnace. The young men were being punished for not bowing down to the king's idol. Still, they had unwavering faith. The boys decided their Heavenly Father was capable of protecting them, no matter the circumstance. One boy stated, "If we are thrown into the blazing furnace, the God we serve is able to deliver us from it, and he will deliver us from Your Majesty's hand" (Daniel 3:17). The key word here is able. The young men determined they were going to worship only one God: the God who was capable of rescuing them, even from an oven of fire! What? Even the strongest Christian might think, "Once we're thrown in, that's it. We're toast. This must be what God has for us." But no. These young men decided to believe their Heavenly Father to be all-powerful and able to do anything but fail. They prayed and they knew their God was coming; and He did come.

In life, we are often placed in life-testing, sometimes life-threating, situations. Not to mention the fact that our fear lens makes conditions appear worse than they are. Still, as a believer in Christ, you can take the heat of absolutely any challenge. God knows all about your distress. He knows when you just can't handle one more dreadful circumstance. You may feel stuck; you are not. You might feel alone; you are not. Call out to Him! God is able to keep you from anything and everything that is against you. He may not come when you want Him. But know that God is able to tread through any waves of danger, destruction, harm, or hurt. He will pick you up out of your personal boat of terror and place your feet on dry land. When in need, when everything else fails, when you have no one and nothing else left, call on Jesus. You may not know exactly how He's going to carry you through. Just know He's coming. He might grab you out, stop the mill, or simply coach you through it. But Daddy's coming. Just know that He is able.

Make It a Habit: *Remind yourself that your Heavenly Father hears your cry and acknowledge that He is able to keep you. Tell Him today, "God, You are able. I know You are able, and I trust You today." Later, when you are busy or tired, stop and tell God (and remind yourself) that He is able by repeating the words above. He will carry you through.*

WE MUST PURSUE HIM!

But seek first his kingdom and his righteousness, and all these things will be given to you as well.
—Matthew 6:33

Have you ever been in a room with someone who, for the most part, forgot you were there? You are sharing what you believe to be a very compelling story. The other person wants to look as if they are listening. Every once in a while, they shoot you an occasional glance from their phone and respond to the last few words they heard you say. I'm not saying this person is acting with malicious intent. Yet somehow it sure feels like it. When this type of situation occurs, the person feeling ignored often turns their conversation towards someone else who appears to be listening, especially if a response is needed to support their position at the end of the discussion. I have found myself on both ends of this scenario. I have stared at my phone knowing my ability to multitask is going to fade and my attention is eventually going to drift completely towards whatever message I believe can't wait. On the other hand, when the shoe is on the other foot, and I'm sharing my two cents (as my mother would say), well, you'd better have more convincing feedback than the predictable response of "Wow!"

I've yet to find someone who likes to be ignored.

Often when God doesn't answer us in the way we believe He should, we get impatient because we are expecting a humanoid response. We may think God is saying "no," or that maybe He's not listening, or even perhaps that He's giving us the silent treatment. When we anticipate that God will respond like we would, but He doesn't, it may put us in the mindset that our relationship is not as sacred as it could be. We may feel like we haven't put God in the position to grant us all that we currently need. If we're not careful, we can actually start to believe that God has us in a time-out because we deserve it. Or worse, that He is flat-out ignoring us. This is when we run the risk of jumping off track and handling things on our own.

Hearing nothing from God can be extremely tricky for many of us. Our moral standards can take a nosedive at this point. We tend to kick into survival mode. We begin to do things like rob Peter to pay Paul. In other words, we use money set aside for one purpose to do something else. This type of action is understandable in many cases, but we often stretch the boundaries of our morals a little further when God is silent in our lives. We sometimes take matters out of God's hands and into our own when we feel our comfortable lifestyle is in jeopardy. While going through life's difficulties, our individual troubles are sometimes magnified, and we feel alone to do whatever we have to do.

For example, we might call a guy considered to be "just a friend" to chat about life's challenges, knowing he'll be saddened by our situation and feel compelled to help financially. We often give up our standards when we feel our backs are against the wall. Or, we might reconnect with a friend whose behavior has always been intolerable, knowing she will always babysit in a crunch. Her lifestyle has always been troublesome; yet when needed, she's "not so bad."

Maybe you've never used these means to solve a situation. Still, you get the point. These are just a few examples of how we as women often lower our standards to survive. Using a guy friend to get a little cash or support doesn't seem harmful since that's what good friends do. He gets the romantic attention he desires, and you receive gas money to get to work next week. The friend either doesn't know you are using him, or he knows and doesn't care because he loves you. Either way, God always knows our intent. In any situation, we must remember His love for us and grant others the same. Everyone wants to secure their future, and God's silence sometimes makes us panic. Still, we must keep in mind, the struggle is not ours; it's the Lord's.

When we pursue God instead of people, God has room to step in and care for us. Matthew 6:33 reminds us that seeking God and all His righteousness brings us all that we will ever need. We don't have to scheme, pretend to be someone else, or put our morals in jeopardy. God has what we want; He has what we need. We can channel our creative hustle in the direction of God, not down the road of manipulation and deceit of those who trust and love us.

How do we chase God and not do what comes naturally? Read or listen to videos that break down God's Word in a way you can understand it. Next, seek a mentor. Ask a woman whose manner and conduct you trust and admire to help guide you in the way of pleasing God and reaching your full purpose. Do whatever you need to do to be the best example you can for your children and/or loved ones. Then try to make sure you share that same wisdom with another woman. It not only feels great to share, but you begin to feel better about yourself and habitually begin to think more and more like God. Make it a habit!

Moving forward: Go after Him! Today, think of small ways to bless a friend who may not have family or a great support system. Sometimes we believe we have to do a lot to make a huge impact in someone's life, but the truth is, every little bit counts.

HIS LOVE IS UNCONDITIONAL!

Therefore, since we have been justified through faith, we have peace with God through our Lord Jesus Christ, through whom we have gained access by faith into this grace in which we now stand. And we boast in the hope of the glory of God. Not only so, but we also glory in our sufferings, because we know that suffering produces perseverance; perseverance, character; and character, hope. And hope does not put us to shame, because God's love has been poured out into our hearts through the Holy Spirit, who has been given to us. You see, at just the right time, when we were still powerless, Christ died for the ungodly.
—Romans 5:1-6

There is no way to participate in church all of your life and not run into drama. Churches are made of families, families of people, and people tend to fill in the gaps with their own thoughts when they don't know all they want to know about you. As a young married woman, I remember being super naive and wondering why some of our friends didn't come around like they used to do. In fact, some actually responded as if they didn't care for my husband and me at all anymore. We loved God and we loved participating at church, and we were absolutely devastated when we heard some of the rumors that were started about us. We tried to move forward. Then the situation went too far, and discussions had to be held. Unfortunately, arguments took place before hearts were mended. But as for me, I was still a little angry at the person who I believed had the maturity to shut down all the mess from the start.

One day, I couldn't help myself. I stared at this person with reckless disregard. I had not let it all go. I had to stop looking and force myself to try and understand. This same day, God told me to look at this individual again. He said, "This time, try to look as I look at you. Walk over there, look at that soul, and say out loud, 'There is nothing you can do to make me stop loving you!'" I couldn't believe God wanted me to repeat this. He actually wanted me to say it out loud to this person! So I did...and I've been saying it to people ever since. I believe God wanted me to realize that loving unconditionally simply means the object of our affection is powerless against the arms of love.

God's Got a Habit : God's Unconditional Love

People cannot make you love them. I was OK with knowing that part. On the other hand, the part I chose to ignore was that people cannot make you stop loving them either. Uh oh! God wanted me to know that when I love, I win. Love is an act that we can set, stop, or continue if we want. If you set your heart to love as God does, no one can make you stop loving people. Like the doors of the church, the arms of our love are usually open. Do we have to be abused by those that we love? No! Absolutely not. Love has boundaries and respectful limits depending on the type of relationship. Still, love often continues long after a bond is broken. Relationships may end, and boundaries may have to change, but love can still remain unconditional.

God has a habit of loving us! He loves us even though we sin against Him daily. Set your mind to love and to teach others how to love you. Be free from handing out judgment. That's up to God. Not everyone can handle love, so you may get hurt in the process. Loving unconditionally gets difficult sometimes. But it can become a habit. Be free enough to love. Keep moving if you must move on from the person that hurt you. But set yourself free enough to love unconditionally.

Make It a Habit: Tell someone today that there is nothing they can do to make you stop loving them. Think about what that looks like for that particular connection in your life. Then do it. You'll be surprised at how many are in need of love without conditions.

GIVE YOUR ALL

Jesus replied: "Love the Lord your God with all your heart and with all your soul and with all your mind."
—Matthew 22:37

Call me cheesy, but I love motivational expressions and hashtags that draw us to an important purpose or cause. Creating expressions and idioms can often make a challenging or boring activity seem interesting. Several social media memes get us charged up and driven to go the extra mile. I respond positively to the phrase, "How do you eat an elephant? One piece at a time." As silly as it sounds, it works for me. Whenever I hear it, I understand that I need to move back, slow down, and proceed one step at a time. Such expressions help us break projects down into small doses of work or common sense. Still, there are instances where no encouraging words can help our situation. Sometimes we just need the raw, naked truth. One of my aunties used to tell us, "Hey...cool your jets, right now!" Everyone in the room knew that meant, "Hey, cool down whatever has your engine revved up; and this is your final warning." No fluff. Just direction.

Jesus often used phrases and parables to guide others. However, He had no problem with giving direction. He gave the pure uncovered truth. In Matthew 22, the Pharisees heard that Jesus put the Sadducees to silence with His answers to their questions. One of the Pharisees asked the Lord Jesus a question of his own: "Which is the greatest commandment?" Jesus said, "Love the Lord your God with all your heart and with all your soul and with all your mind" (Matthew 22:37). Jesus doesn't use a parable or expression here. Jesus reminds the Pharisees that they have one job: love Christ with all their heart, soul, and mind. No sugar to help the medicine go down. Jesus got straight to the point. For believers today, this means we too have one job: love God with all we've got! But how do we give God everything? What do we give a God that has everything? Well, for starters, we give Him exactly what He says He wants: our all!

It's been said that 80% of commitment is just showing up. The rest is being consistent. In other words, just get started. The next time, show up and do it again. You have an 80% chance of fulfilling any commitment if you just show up. Just get started! You cannot eat an elephant one piece at a time if you never make it to the table. Show up and then you can start working on the pieces to eventually give your all.

I often remind myself that I can imagine encouraging as many people as I want, but no one will be moved if I don't write it down. I have to get started somewhere. Thinking about it can only take us so far. To start giving God our all, perhaps we can connect with Him through prayer first thing in the morning. Before I drink water or go to the restroom each morning, I read at least one scripture. The verse may or may not become a part of my morning devotion. However, my goal is to make sure that the first item my eyes work to see is the Word of God in the morning. I sit up, grab my phone, touch my Bible app, and look for the Word. This means I've started my day with my eyes on God. Now, I can pray and keep the line of communication open all day long.

If you're like me, you can answer one phone call and that conversation can change the course of your day before you even eat breakfast. Take control of where your time goes. Create a routine that will make sure you focus your entire being on God. Jesus never told the Pharisees to give just a part of themselves if "their all" was too much to give. It's basically give all or nothing! For good reason too. When we each give our all to God individually, we come to worship service with the idea of just getting closer to Him. This sets an awesome foundation for unity among your inner circle and church family. It is extremely important to spend time loving on God each day. It is a direct command from God Himself. If you find yourself having gone too long without talking to God, don't run from Him. I've been there and I know you can't outrun Him. He's actually waiting to hear from you. God wants your love, remember? Jesus said it is the most important commandment. Our love is so indispensable to God that Jesus literally deems it the most essential of our priorities. What an honor it is for the God of everything to want the affection of little ol' us. Show God love. Pray for compassion and forgiveness and give your all to Him, one prayer at a time.

Make It a Habit: Give God everything you've got by starting your day with Him. Give your affection and attention. Give little by little, all day long. Give yourself an 80% chance to succeed each day by just showing up before Him!

DELIGHT YOURSELF IN LIVING FOR GOD!

Take delight in the Lord, and he will give you the desires of your heart. Commit your way to the Lord; trust in him and he will do this: He will make your righteous reward shine like the dawn, your vindication like the noonday sun. —Psalm 37:4-6

When my husband, John, and I first got married, I constantly thought of different ways to show him I loved him. When we had disagreements, I purposely gave genuine hugs and smiles to let him know that while the issue at hand made me upset, we are always "good." His way of displaying the same sentiment was (and still is) to say, "Don't forget, we still go together." In other words, "We will always date each other no matter how this plays out."

Small gestures like those help partners find pleasure in each other's company, even when days are tough and attitudes flare. But what takes place when these tactics get old and no longer seem to work? What can you do when your go-to solutions are dry and ineffective? This is a great time to get to know your loved one again. It's the perfect time to think about all that is great about the relationship and build on that. You can literally design a good time in the presence of that other person, just as you did when the relationship was new. You know, back when just the thought of being in your mate's view caused you to smile with reckless glee? When John and I were dating prior to marriage, I didn't care if we got together just to play Tic-Tac-Toe. I just wanted to be in the room with him. This is what is meant by the statement, "Delight yourself in the Lord" (Psalm 37:4). We can take pleasure in just the presence of the Lord.

David wrote Psalm 37 in his old age. It is a reminder that we all have more to give, as well as a guide to growing and living for Christ. Verses 4-6 promote development since the rest of the Psalm speaks of caring lightly for the things around us that will fade with time. Nothing of this world lasts forever. The shoes we love will ultimately go out of style. Our bodies will age, and our skin will inevitably pay homage to gravity. The emotions of friends and family will fluctuate. The strength of our adversaries will weaken. Yet, there is One who is consistent and righteous. God is our only true endless constant! His grace is endless while His mercy never ends!

Considering these things, David submits to us the wise eternal decision to put our trust and joy solely in the Lord! Sure, verse 4 of Psalm 37 does teach us that God will give us the desires of our heart. Hallelujah! But this is specifically a bonus, my friend. We will get our desires as we align our hearts with God. Still, the emphasis of the text particularly leans towards the fact that all other ground is sinking sand. Outside of God and His will lies shaky territory. Fixing on the triumphs of our enemies will lead us nowhere. Scrolling through social media to check up on the haves and have-nots can only amuse for a while, but looking back over yesteryear and remembering how God healed your body will bring joy to you and the Lord! Just gazing over yesterday and considering how your Heavenly Father kept you from having an emotional breakdown in front of everyone at work or the grocery store will delight you while pleasing Him!

If you're feeling as if your relationship is dulling, take action. As we grow more and more familiar with God, it is important to recall why we fell in love with Him in the first place. You know, back when just recognizing His presence was enough to make us smile. This is the time to remember God's promises and build on that.

Make It a Habit: *Remember His love for you. Create a spark in your living by telling the Lord how you trust, believe, and appreciate Him. Then, think about it... there is something God wants you to pursue. You may be the only one who knows. Still that's enough. Write it down. Make His desire your desire. Big or small, pray about it, write it down, and praise God in advance! Be sure to give God the glory and acknowledge your own hard work after it comes to pass.*

YOU CAN'T
PLEASE EVERYBODY

DAY 6

Do not be afraid of those who kill the body but cannot kill the soul. Rather, be afraid of the One who can destroy both soul and body in hell. —Matthew 10:28

Western civilization may not revere them as much, but several cultures still cling to the advice and counsel of the aged. Some societies still deem the guidance of our elders as priceless and immeasurable. Do the seniors of the world mess up and sometimes get life wrong too? Of course. However, experience is one of our best teachers, and teachers often tell great stories. Countless nations embrace the notion that older men and women hold the key to practical wealth and longevity. I agree wholeheartedly. My grandmother's counsel was always on point. I would often confide in her about one thing or another. I'd tiptoe my way softly towards my opinion or concern and Grandma would always skip straight to the point.

One time in particular, I remember her interrupting my statement with, "Well, one thing for certain... two things for sure; you can't please everybody all of the time." Grandma knew I had a problem with disappointing others and that I hated to say no. She knew it was impossible to survive as an adult with that attitude. Consequently, she did her best to help me understand that I was trying to do something that was impossible and essentially a waste of good intent. How did Gram know this rationale or way of thinking was a misuse of time? Simply experience. Gram knew that the people we try to please are often satisfied for a little while, but never entirely. People change their minds and life directions incessantly without warning. To placate them, you'll have to fall in line and do the same. For me, that would be a mind-numbing existence. Such a goal is completely unreachable and intolerable. Unfortunately, I still have to remind myself to say no and remember the instruction Grandma gave me.

When Moses went to the top of Mount Sinai in Exodus 24, the people of Israel indicated they understood why Moses had to go away and that they were willing to do whatever God wanted them to do. But when Moses stayed at the top of the mountain longer than they expected in Chapter 32, the people begged Moses' brother Aaron to help them create idols and fulfill their needs. They didn't want to wait on Moses or God. They were furious at the leaders and the process that was taking so much longer than they expected. While Moses was on the mountain, God told him that the people below were going against God's plan. God told Moses to go down the mountain as He burnt His rage against the people and consumed them (Exodus 32:10). Moses asked for grace on his people's behalf, and God granted it.

The bottom line is, Moses did not please the Israelites all of the time. God Himself did not even please them most of the time. Moses brought some gratification to the people. Still, they turned on him when he took too long to do what they required. The Israelites didn't just oppose what was going on; we could understand that. Disagreement is a part of life. The people went against God's will to get what they wanted. Think about it. The people we often work so hard to please are the ones who are so brazenly uncompromising later.

In Matthew 10, Jesus explains that understanding this principle is key to successful discipleship since those who share the gospel will be persecuted for His sake anyway. He tells the disciples in verse 28: "Do not be afraid of those who kill the body but cannot kill the soul. Rather, be afraid of the One who can destroy both soul and body in hell." In other words, the only one you have to fear is the Lord. He is the only one who can change your eternal end. Gram used to put it this way: "Don't worry about them [other people]; they don't have a heaven or hell to put you in." Yes Gram! Why waste time travailing over whether or not you are making people happy, when happiness is only based on happenstance? Happiness is based on what happens. We can't wait for happenstance or people to complete us. Happiness only lasts for a while. What we really want for our ourselves, our friends, and our family is joy. Joy unspeakable that only God can provide. Joy that only God can take away.

Like Moses, you don't have to be influenced by observers. Keep doing what lines up with the Word of God for you and your family. Hold your ground and stay on your own path—not to instigate or intentionally provoke disputes with others, but to simply make sure that you are concentrated on God and His end. Sure, it's satisfying to fulfill another's wants, but not to the point that it compromises God's mission through you. I often have to tell myself not to forget why I believe what I believe. God saved me from myself and sent me in a challenging direction. Everyone needs the opportunity to hear from God and step in the direction He grants. If you've begun a journey that you know is God-aimed, don't agonize when those that began with you seem to turn away. Don't fret when your supporters decrease. It's human nature. God will grant the increase.

Make It a Habit: Steer away from constantly proving your point or innocence to people. Individuals will make up their own minds. Make up yours. Let it go! Remember, you can lead a horse to water, but you can't make him drink! You're welcome. ~Grandma

---

X-CAPE

No temptation has overtaken you except what is common to mankind. And God is faithful; he will not let you be tempted beyond what you can bear. But when you are tempted, he will also provide a way out so that you can endure it. **—1 Corinthians 10:13**

When my GPS instructs me to take a shifty-looking exit at night, I'm relieved when a street sign confirms I'm actually going in the right direction. Being lost feels terrible. Your freedom appears so close, yet so far away. Think with me for a moment. Have you ever been on your way to a place you've been before, but just can't remember how to get there because it's been a while since you've been in the area? You believe the map app you're using is probably correct, but the sights you're seeing and the road you're traveling just don't feel right. Suddenly, a road appears that leads you out of the horrifying loop of darkness. You make it out, and dramatically praise God as if He has just come down and pulled you out of the gates of hell before the flames touched your feet. Sometimes the fear of getting lost makes us feel as if death is on our heels. This can force us to create our own escape. It can scare us into taking the wrong road just to experience comfort and familiarity again.

In 1 Corinthians 10:13, Paul guarantees the people of Corinth that the roads of temptation before them are the same trails that have enticed mankind forever. Their enticements were not new but common. Paul also encourages the people of Corinth to understand that when tempted, God will make a way out so that they may endure. Thank God for a means of escape. Yes, our Heavenly Father will make a way out.

How do we choose the right road when so many appear promising? How do you choose the right exit when they all seem to have potential? Well, occasionally, we just have to go "old school" by taking it slow and reading the signs—just like we used to do before GPS systems were around. Every now and again we have to stop, relax, and back up from our decisions to take the personal panic out of making the correct choice. It's time to take off the armor of anxiety to see the bigger picture. One way to do this is to write down the issue at hand. Your life choices are as significant as, or even more important than, any plan you would execute for your job or business. Thus, design and preparation are warranted. You must also write down the end you imagine. When we do this and stick to it, we put ourselves in a better position to grasp our objectives.

Let's say you want a personal trainer who pushes you to take risk and loves outdoors; yet your current trainer dislikes adventure and only makes use of a few pieces of equipment in the gym. Eventually, you'll need to get off the road to monotony before you find yourself skipping workouts due to boredom or disinterest. Even if the trainer is a great person or friend, you can't ignore the signs of incompatibility and conflicting preferences when you are trying to improve your life. You will not get the results you imagine. Your destination matters. Make your plan and stick with it.

Where fear of abuse is a concern, safety planning is necessary. If changing directions in your situation is potentially dangerous for you or your family, seek resources. If you are in a relationship and believe you are in danger, seek help immediately. Many churches are full of excellent resources and referrals. Don't let "not knowing" what to do stop you from taking the road to safety. It may be tough, but you can get help, my friend. God will make a way for you to endure and get out. Those seeking help from immediate danger should always call 911 or local police before taking any other path.

Remember, Paul said that whatever is challenging you has tempted someone else before. We all need help at one point or another. Your symptoms may present themselves differently, but someone has been where you are. It's OK to reach out for support. Remember that God will make a way out. I like to refer to these ways out as Xcapes. The first letter of the Greek word Christos is translated into the English alphabet as the letter X. It is the symbol for the name of Christ. (It is also why some abbreviate Christmas as Xmas.) You don't have to wander around feeling lost in the dark. Slow down and think it through so that you can see the signs clearly. There is an exit already in place. God has an Xcape in mind for you.

Further reading: *For another example of an Xcape, see 1 Samuel 23:26-29 (David's Xcape from Saul).*

WEEK 2:
4:4

THE WORD IS THE KEY TO SURVIVAL

Jesus answered, "It is written: Man does not live on bread alone, but on every word that comes from the mouth of God." —Matthew 4:4

I remember being a preteen and hanging out outside with family and friends of the same age for hours. Sometimes we'd hang out so long we literally couldn't think of anything else to do. Every once in a while, someone would say, "Let's play Truth or Dare." Remember that game? It's the one where you either have to tell the truth in response to whatever question is asked or someone can dare you to do anything and you have to do it. For some reason, a quick streak of panic would come over me whenever we all agreed to play. It was as if the game were somehow going to change my life if I didn't have interesting answers or complete the dare someone suggested. I never knew why I felt like I had to play. I do know that I was extremely shy growing up. I was very private as well. Still, I was self-confident. After all, the women in my family raised us to be self-assured. Yet, I played Truth or Dare because of what the other children might think if I didn't.

If I'm honest, every once in a while, I still do this. I agree to do tasks or take on responsibilities that aren't necessarily mine to execute. Why do any of us do this? Why do we do things we don't have to do? I'm sure there are many reasons we compromise our standards during each day. For myself, there is one I hate to admit. It is the notion of pleasing others. Even though I'm aware of my inclination to do this, I do it every now and again. I'm excited to share that the book of Matthew has helped me fall for this temptation less and less as I've grown older.

In Matthew 4, Satan presents Jesus with what I perceive to be the most dangerous game of Truth or Dare in history. God sends Jesus to fast in the wilderness for 40 days and 40 nights. Towards the end of this period, Satan appears and tries to tempt Jesus since He has been without food for so long. Satan dares Jesus to turn stones into bread to show that Jesus is the son of God. To this Jesus answers, in verse 4, "It is written: Man does not live on bread alone, but on every word that comes from the mouth of God." There are many lessons in this statement.

For instance, Jesus lets Satan know that His life is actually sustained by the Word of God, not just bread and water. But what I love the most about Jesus' response is the idea that He doesn't waste time entertaining Satan's advances by making qualifying statements such as, "I could do it, but I won't." I believe Jesus does this because He has nothing to prove. Yes, Jesus could have responded with interesting comments about all that He could do, but He kept the focus on God. This was my issue with playing Truth or Dare. I always wanted to prove I wasn't scared. But, if the game was no fun to me, I simply didn't have to play. There was really nothing to gain. It was a game. Jesus was so unruffled by Satan's advances. He knew the devil talked a good game. He simply dismissed Satan's dare with truth.

Sometimes we respond in agreement too quickly to demonstrate the well-rounded life we claim to live. We often compromise during small conversations to keep the peace in our friendships and to show how relatable we are. Of course, Jesus wants us to have peace. His Word is persistent about that. But keep in mind, peace is often interrupted by promotion. In the situation above, Jesus fought against proving anything to Satan since Christ Himself was gradually being promoted to die for our sins and take His position in heaven. The Word is the key to our survival, not man's opinions or priorities. We cannot just take on work because it's for a good cause.

Consider your reason for playing along with other people's games and ask yourself what you'll learn or teach others through the experience. Throughout Matthew 4, Jesus continues to deny Satan's advances by using the Word of God. It would be just three years later that people were hollering for Christ to save Himself instead of going to the cross: yet another game of Truth or Dare. Christ focused on the bigger picture. He again had nothing to prove, but a mission to accomplish. The promotion to the cross brought no peace to Christ's body, but it gave salvation to the body of Christ, the church. Sticking with the truth is a good habit to learn.

Think Better, Do Better: Remember, you have nothing to prove today. When tempted, like Jesus did, stand on the Word of God and make it a habit.

REJOICE IN THE LORD

Rejoice in the Lord always. I will say it again: Rejoice!
—Philippians 4:4

At first glance, or even after several readings, some instructions of the Bible may seem highly unreasonable. A deeper understanding of the context and learning of the author's intent can help us understand what was meant and why it was instructed at the time it was written. Biblical advice can be hard to adhere to if we don't look for deeper meaning. For instance, Paul writes in Philippians 4:4, "Rejoice in the Lord always. I will say it again: Rejoice!" At first glimpse, one might wonder, "How can we rejoice all the time with everything that is going on in the world today?" There are so many missing children, senseless killings, and starving families all over the world. There is even enough trouble on our own plates that it's hard to donate or volunteer sometimes. I myself have said this to God:

> "Lord, I know You know how much I can bear.
> I know You allowed these things in my life to

happen at this very time, but I don't think I need to tell You that I've had enough misfortune right now, God. I am tired and so over these circumstances. I have to admit I am ready to come out of this tribulation, Father. I need You. But most of all, I want Your will to be done."

Have you ever had a similar conversation with God? It's OK. Our Heavenly Father knows how we feel even when we don't disclose it. Hard times are just that...hard! It's tough to watch the local news. How are we expected to rejoice all the time when things aren't always rejoice-able, if you will?

If we consider just some of what Paul went through before he'd written these words to the Philippians, we'll see that he writes from a place of experience. In fact, Paul was sending this call to rejoice from a Roman jail, where he'd been persecuted and badly beaten for being a Christian. Paul, of all people, had to know that every moment of life is not a cause to celebrate. Yet, he declares that all should rejoice! Looking even closer at Paul's request, we can find that he asked us not to rejoice in our heartbreaks, calamities, mishaps, or tough blows. He instructs us to rejoice in the Lord!

This changes the entire meaning of "Rejoice always," my friends. It means we can recognize our situation without glorifying it. We can simply change our minds and transfer the glory to God. That's all. For example, you might say, "I don't have a dime right now; thank God I went shopping on Monday and have dinner for the rest of the week." Or, "I feel terrible today, but at least it's Saturday and I do not have to call off from work." These accounts sound simple. But they are actually announcements that remind us that our words dictate our witness. Our words tell our story. We all feel like complaining sometimes. Simply stating that you have no money is a complaint. But describing that you are low on cash and still have food for the week explains your reality while giving glory to God. It says, "I don't have much money now, but I have what I need." It takes the focus off your struggle and magnifies the fact that God is your provider! We can identify our issues while rejoicing because we have Christ through it all. It is exciting just to know that our Heavenly Father sees and He cares! He knows your name, and on top of it all, He cares. Hallelujah!

Paul moves on in Philippians 4, verses 5-6, to tell us to let our gentleness shine through, to be anxious for nothing, but in every situation, by prayer and petition, with thanksgiving, to present our requests to God. When times are tough as a result of bad decision making or the damage done to you from the words of a spiteful person, rejoice and let your gentleness show through. Do this so that others might observe your situation and celebrate. God is a faithful wonderful God who knows how much you can handle. Grip on to the fact that He cares about what you are going through. Whatever it is, rejoice; again I say, rejoice!

Make It a Habit: *In all things, glorify the Lord, not your situation!*

GOD IS JUDGE

My conscience is clear, but that does not make me innocent. It is the Lord who judges me. **—1 Corinthians 4:4**

I've worked with youth for many years. Children of all ages. One statement I often hear young children say to teachers is this: "You can't tell me what to do; only my mom or dad can tell me what to do." While moms and dads probably are the ones who give their children the most directives, this pronouncement seems to be some sort of statute that many children either assume or are actually being told by their parents. Either way, most seem to believe it is a pass to do what they want since, in their minds, no one outside of their parents can tell them what to do.

For me, this theory is a recipe for disaster. It might feel good to think that nobody can tell us how and when to do anything. Realistically, this just isn't so. The prison system is filled with people who don't like to respond to authority. The system is also of course full of some wrongfully convicted inmates, and not all prisoners are in jail for disrespecting authority. But some people simply don't like to obey the law. Some believe that no one has the right to enforce regulations upon them, ever. Some who think this way now have officers telling them exactly what to do all day and night. It is sad, but true. Several government, state, and local guidelines are outdated and even discriminatory, but most general systems are set in place to keep us safe. Parents, please let your children know sooner than later that there are systems and rules that exist outside of your home, and there are consequences for not adhering to those rules or obeying the authorities that uphold them.

There is another statement I've heard as a sort of waiver to bad behavior by children and adults alike. It's the phrase "Only God can judge me." I've heard it mentioned jokingly but also during heated debates. It is often used to dodge criticism. It can also mean "I sin, but so do you." Either way, I get this one. Paul makes a similar statement in 1 Corinthians 4:4. He says, "My conscience is clear, but that does not make me innocent. It is the Lord who judges me." Paul doesn't use his statement to suggest that he can do whatever he wants and let God judge. In fact, many believe Paul shares his wisdom as a way to advise the people of Philippi to stop wasting time judging what each person is doing since God has the final say. Paul understood that we have freedom from guilt if we have truly given ourselves to Christ just as we are. In other words, we were given the gift of life eternal. We did not earn it because our sin was more palatable to God than some other sins. We inherited it. Salvation was gifted. Not one of us is higher or more worthy than another.

Honestly, I used to have a love-hate relationship with Paul's teachings. His instruction can be a bit heavy handed. Over time, I've learned to appreciate Paul's perspective more and more. For instance, in verse 3 of Corinthians 4, Paul lets us know that he doesn't care if others judge him. Seems arrogant at first. But he then moves on to say, "I don't even judge myself." No overconfidence here. Paul is actually warning us not to even waste time on judging ourselves. It is not until we get to verse 4 that Paul sums all of this up by saying, "It is the Lord who judges me." Paul was guilt-free because Jesus already accepted him as he was. This is awesome news to those who follow Christ. Paul's words are made to give us hope in God's mercy, not an excuse to escape man's judgment. We don't have to audition to be on God's team. It is a gift. The gift of relationship with Him. One that only God can judge.

Think Better, Do Better: *Remember, not even you have the right to judge you. God has the final say in your life. So leave guilt at home today. Just leave home without it.*

NO LONGER
ADDICTED TO YOU

They are surprised that you do not join them in their reckless, wild living, and they heap abuse on you. **—1 Peter 4:4**

Our minds and bodies are often our worst enemies. Individuals who have recovered from substance abuse and/or physical addictions are heroes of a special kind in my book. Whether they've been clean five days or five years, I'm a fan. It takes a special type of person to fight against the daily cravings the body has been convinced it needs to survive. Just imagine what the survivors of addictions endure on a daily basis. Envision living with your senses striving daily to reach the ecstasy they once grasped, while still recovering from the damage it once caused. Beating an obsession is difficult. However, what may be just as challenging is the backlash you can receive from those who were with you while you did what you used to do.

1 Peter 4:4 says this: "They are surprised that you do not join them in their reckless, wild living, and they

heap abuse on you." Peter made this statement concerning those who were living wildly and not following Christ. He was writing to the Christians in the various regions of the Roman Empire. Peter was sending word that whoever suffers in the body will be done with sin, just like Christ. Even though this is great eternal news, Peter tells the people that those who are still living in debauchery, lust, and idolatry are going to be surprised you are no longer living that way and will begin to persecute you on earth. Sometimes people fall back into what they gave up because someone around them keeps pulling them back into the act. This can be true with any contaminated connection such as alcoholism, drug addiction, toxic relationships, or work fixations. This is why we occasionally have to let go of those people who are associated with our sins so that we can move forward towards the will of God.

When you are no longer addicted to your past, some are going to be surprised you've moved on and will draw their own conclusions as to why. When my boyfriend (now husband) gave his live to Christ when we were younger, many assumed his Christianity was due to my encouragement. Of course, I wanted better for him. I did inspire him to go for his goals.

But he and Christ met without my introduction. In fact, his decision to go beyond his normal sights was an inspiration of God that I never could have designed. Since he made a decision to let go, change paths, and think better, I moved forward and gave my life to Christ as well. I wanted to have that kind of relationship with the God that could make a guy like him address his past and embrace the idea of a new future.

Once YOU let go of what once held you down, you'll be able to reach out and explore other options. Just go for it. Tell your past, "I'm no longer addicted to you!" Respect your time and appreciate the journey.

Make It a Habit: Don't let what you'll miss keep you from what you'll meet.

BALANCE IT

For everything God created is good, and nothing is to be rejected if it is received with thanksgiving...
—1 Timothy 4:4

No-carb, protein, cabbage soup, low fat—these are just a few of the diets that are among us these days. There are of course many, many more plans designed to help us eat sparingly and get healthy. I honestly don't think I can count the number of diets and alternative food lifestyles I've entertained in my lifetime. Some worked. Some didn't. But less food always seemed like the top choice.

As a borderline diabetic for most of my years, I've spent a good bit of my life trying to find foods and beverages with little to no sugar that don't taste like paper. I now, however, have trained my taste buds not to believe sweetness is the key to taste. A nutritionist once told me that for me, what I was eating was not really the issue. She explained that I need to add different types of foods to my menu and eat them more often. She mentioned what another nutritionist once told me: "Balance is the key. Stop restricting foods and start balancing them."

In 1 Timothy 4:4, Paul says, "For everything God created is good, and nothing is to be rejected if it is received with thanksgiving..." Every single thing God created is great. The earth, the sky, the clouds, the trees, fruit, even humans. All are wonderful when God put them together. It is our modifications, variations, wastefulness, reckless living, and crossbreeding that tip the scales of the world from nourishing to harmful. The changes we as humans have made to make food convenient and more plentiful have also altered their original purpose and nutritional value. Still, it doesn't mean what God made wasn't good initially. Some companies alter food to make more money. Sometimes it's literally to make food more digestible or appealing. Either way is the human way because we are not perfect. Figuring out how to take care of these bodies God has given us can be tricky. I've struggled with digestive issues for a long time. I haven't eaten beef or pork since my stomach started responding negatively towards it 23 years ago. I've tried dieting, journaling, being a vegetarian—you name it, I've tried it. But I haven't given up on the fact that God can take away all of my digestive issues if He desires. I have learned to channel my obsession away from my eating habits and what my body "looks like" towards God. Some days this goes well. Other days...I'm not sure how the sweets ended up in the kitchen. But it's all good. God made it all good.

It's definitely important not to eat too much of the wrong stuff. There are everyday foods (such as fruits and veggies), and sometime foods (like sweets and fast foods). Again, balance is the key. This is tough. God knows this. So He gives us a chance to help ourselves before we dine. Paul tells us that everything is good if we receive it with thanksgiving. In other words, when we bless our food before we eat it, the blessing actually occurs when we say thank you! This is so great! The fact that sometimes I eat on the run makes this so very wonderful. Perhaps we don't always need all of the words we throw in front of our thanks when we pray; could it just be that the gratitude itself is where the blessing lies? I mean, of course, just thinking about the goodness of God makes us want to adorn Him with words of praise when we pray. That's different. I mean, maybe we don't have to throw all of the traditional stuff in (before we say thanks for the food) just because we've been hearing it all our lives. We can be comfortable with knowing everything God makes is good when we use it for the purpose it was intended; and we give thanks when we indulge. We can loosen up and genuinely say, "thank you," and God takes it from there. The blessing is in our thanksgiving! Our job is to just balance our intake and give it to all to Him.

Think Better, Do Better: *You could worry about what you eat every minute of the day. But you don't have to do that. Remember, everything God created is good. Pray for your individual diet, health, and wellness. Gain knowledge of foods, listen to your body, think about what the good decisions are, and make them; but please...don't sweat the small stuff. Bon appétit!*

HE > WORLD

You, dear children, are from God and have overcome them, because the one who is in you is greater than the one who is in the world. —*1 John 4:4*

Since we can communicate across the world in seconds, we get to see all that's evil or glamorous in the world just as, or right after, it happens. When you see this constantly, it almost feels as if immorality is winning. It really seems as if evil is on top when those whom we believe are responsible are seemingly prosperous and successful. The world these days appears so powerful. So much violence and selfishness going on all around us. For me, sometimes it feels as if I wake up with the weight of the world on my shoulders. My to-do list is large, and everything on it seems necessary for my life and family to progress. This is when it is important to remember that we are not alone.

The Roman emperor Marcus Aurelius once said, "The best revenge is not to be like your enemy." Being a Christian means we have a jumpstart on being different since we are striving to be more like Christ. God did not just create us; He lives in us. "You, dear children, are from God and have overcome them, because the one who is in you is greater than the one who is in the world (1 John 4:4). Right here, God lets us know that we win, and it is because of Him we do so.

Many scholars believe John was writing 1 John chapter 4 to a group of Christians who were battling false teachers from within their own faith. He wanted the Christians to know that even this sort of evil would not prevail. God is always with the believer. God is bigger than anything our day could bring. The God we love, serve, respect, and follow is far greater than he that is in this world. Sometimes you have nothing else to stand on. No prediction of the future. No one to tell you your latter will be greater than your former. You just have what God has promised you; and really...that's enough. John says we are overcomers simply because we have God's Spirit living on the inside of us. When you gave your life to God, you took on more than you could ever imagine. Big ideas and goals, sure. But you also took on the power, the boldness, the blood of the victorious, and the determination of one who has already tasted victory! Yes, that's who you are. Embrace it, allow it, don't run from it. You are not being humble by denying yourself the joy of celebrating the win before you cross the finish line. Celebrate because the God who lives in you is greater than the largest deadline and the greatest obstacle. Hallelujah and amen! Have fun knowing that God is with you today. Nope, young lady, you are not alone.

Make It a Habit: When you start your day, eat your lunch, and on your way back home, try reminding and saying to yourself, "Greater is He that is in me than he that is in the world." God created you the way He wanted you, and He is still with you because He loves you. Make it a habit to know you are not alone.

ENDLESS OPPORTUNITIES

Pray that I may proclaim it clearly, as I should.
—Colossians 4:4

Good day! It is a new day. We have the opportunity to share God's Word and goodness one more time! You've heard the phrase "sharing is caring." It's true. Let me hear about a sale anywhere, and I am telling everyone I know. When strangers say, "I love your dress," that's it...I'll tell them how much it was, what department store I got it from, and which location to be specific. When it comes to living, I try to show my care for others that they might see my good works and glorify Him. Still, sometimes you have to just look someone in the eye, tell them about the Lord, and pray for them right there.

When I was younger—19 to be exact—I belonged to an evangelism team led by a minister from my church. My husband and I were engaged back then and we both joined the group with big-time zeal and excitement. We were new Christians and wanted to tell the world about the God we met and loved.

Our team went through lessons, fasted, prayed, role played, and hit the streets of the Lincoln & Larimer section of Pittsburgh, Pennsylvania. We couldn't wait. But something happened when we got there. Our leader had a microphone (What? Where did that come from?) and people were watching her speak as if she were telling everyone to run because aliens were coming to take over every mall in America. I just froze. One onlooker walked up to me, asked what I believed, and my mouth got dry as if I'd swallowed a spoonful of peanut butter. I couldn't believe it. But with each new person I spoke to, I got better. I relaxed and spoke more clearly. It was simply that, for me, this was a new level of sharing God's Word.

Now, imagine yourself at Paul's level of evangelism. You are writing while in chains, asking the people of God to pray, not that you be set free, not that you escape, and not that those who have imprisoned you fail, but that you have more opportunities to share the gospel while you are behind bars. Yes, this a different set of skills. This is a man truly focused on his Lord and Savior for real. In verse 3 of Colossians 4, Paul says, "And pray for us, too, that God may open a door for our message, so that we may proclaim the mystery of Christ, for which I am in chains." Then he states, "Pray that I may proclaim it clearly, as I should." It is important to tell people about your special relationship with God as only you can tell it. So many of us are searching for love in all the wrong places, and God can help. You don't need a microphone, an evangelist team, or a handwritten guide. You are everything! No one can be who you are to the world and no one can explain what God means to you.

Think Better, Do Better: *We have to be wise in how we promote God's image to others. We can have respectful conversations. Today is a good day to tell your story!*

WEEK 3:
PB&J: Petty, Broke & Jealous

LOVE BEYOND WORDS

DAY
15

Likewise, the tongue is a small part of the body, but it makes great boasts. Consider what a great forest is set on fire by a small spark. The tongue also is a fire, a world of evil among the parts of the body. **—James 3:5-6**

There is a woman I've known for years who absolutely loves the book of James. She particularly admires James 3:5-6. This lady (we'll call her Mrs. Smith) used to quote this verse to me and other young ladies all the time. I knew James chapter 3 warned us about speaking harshly to others. Therefore, I could not comprehend why Mrs. Smith kept reminding me of this when it wasn't even my style to hurt people using severe language. "Reading people," or telling people what you think of them without care, is not a trait of my character. Honestly, Mrs. Smith's attitude was unwarranted and increasingly annoying to me.

Eventually, I began a class under her leadership. I soon realized my pettiness was permitting me to see the situation only at face value. Mrs. Smith's reason for mentioning James 3 to me wasn't because I was rude to anyone; nor did she think I had the tendency to be so. Her reminding me of the tongue's power was her way of training me since she believed God was calling me to a greater role in leadership. Mrs. Smith wanted me to be aware of what could possibly become a challenge in the future. She assured me that her quoting the book of James to other young women was due to her struggle with controlling her own words. She mentioned that warning young people about the influence of the tongue kept her from making slight and petty comments in response to the ignorance of others. Mrs. Smith was essentially telling herself to keep calm and remember God. When I heard her teach and confess these things, I was relieved. I once thought Mrs. Smith was utterly petty and committed to wearing me thin. After hearing her introduction to our class, I realized we were simply being led by a woman who was willing to be transparent to keep us from using words to destroy people.

Have you ever accused someone of being obsessed with minor issues and later found that the one who was actually doing so was you? I have sipped from the petty cup and eventually learned that I was the one creating an excuse to hold someone accountable for something small and irrelevant. I was hurt, so I put up a wall and charged the other person with the accusation of pettiness so I that I had a reason to stay away from them. In other words, I projected my narrowmindedness onto someone else. That's terribly dangerous and petty.

James 3:5-6 reminds us that our tongues are powerful. So powerful that the author likens the tongue to a spark that sets a forest on fire. Small but lethal. Controlling your words is a great undertaking to master, especially during those times when others are actually being rude or offensive. You believe they are doing their best to annoy you and provoke you. They have pettiness dripping from their being and you are trying to gather the words to even pray. We often feel we have the right to set someone straight in these situations. But that's really not our job. We should always share knowledge from a place of love.

Rarely is our job to correct. Our God is big enough to handle pettiness and everything else. If this reminds you of a particular personal relationship or person you've been dodging, and you know God is calling you to take the high road, think about praying and reaching out in the spirit of love. It's not too late. Sometimes we have to sacrifice our pride to obey God. This is merely a part of allowing Him lordship over our lives. When you pray, the Holy Spirit can bring ideas as to how you can work on relationships like these. You can do it. Don't let small issues keep you from those you really love and miss. Let's make it a petty-less day!

Make It a Habit: Add this to your morning prayer: "Help me to respond today...in all situations, as You desire, Lord. I want to be aware of my words on Your behalf. Help me strive for love that is above and beyond the words I want to say. In Jesus' name, Amen."

ONGOING CONTENTMENT

I am not saying this because I am in need, for I have learned to be content whatever the circumstances. I know what it is to be in need, and I know what it is to have plenty. I have learned the secret of being content in any and every situation, whether well fed or hungry, whether living in plenty or in want. I can do all this through him who gives me strength.
— *Philippians 4:11-13*

While sitting in a park, a woman said to her friend, "I used to drive that bus every day and wish that I could sit with my dog in this park. Now I sit in this park wishing I could drive that bus again." This feeling is all too familiar to so many of us. Sometimes we are just not satisfied. We want something other than what we have, or we simply want a little more than we have at the moment. Does this mean we are ungrateful? Probably not. Most of us are thankful for the positions we are in, things we've done, and even future opportunities. More often than not, the grass just seems greener on the other side. What we don't have seems so attractive, especially when so many others have it. We usually don't want what's theirs; we want our own. It is far too easy to become envious when someone else has more.

I find myself being content with one situation or another, but that gratification occasionally fades away. Sometimes the excitement of getting what you want is short-lived. Contentment can come and go like the satisfaction you get from having a good meal after waiting too long to eat. You become hangry (angry because you're hungry), you eat, you are happy, and now you crave something sweet for dessert. The thrill is gone, and you are on to wanting something else. It seems we are often content until the next offer is on the table.

Lasting contentment, however—the kind that comes from allowing Christ to be Lord of your life—is the kind of satisfaction Paul speaks of in the book of Philippians chapter 4 verses 11-13. Paul was writing while in confinement. His circumstances were not livable, and certainly not satisfying. Yet, Paul said he learned how to be content in whatever state he was in at the time. He explained how he knew abundance and was no stranger to being poor. Still, he doesn't express any jealousy of those on the outside. Despite it all, Paul was satisfied knowing God was with him wherever he went. This is the one thing no one can take away from us. We are blessed with God's presence and that is sufficient.

It is OK to be progressive and strive to do more and go further than you've ever been. God never asked us to know Him and do nothing else. On the contrary. In John 14:12 Jesus says, "Very truly I tell you, whoever believes in me will do the works I have been doing, and they will do even greater things than these, because I am going to the Father." Jesus said we'll do more than He. What? Yes, Jesus said this. Why? It's because He is going to be with the Father on our behalf. Just as a director sets the setting so that we might see palm leaves blowing and ocean waves crashing behind the characters as they speak, this too is the set-up of our lives. We can have other experiences while keeping our focus on God.

Creating our life setting is important. We gather education and life deeds that eventually set the scene for our stories, while focusing on God as He speaks love, joy, guidance, and peace into our lives! That's it. We can be content in whatever state we are in, just like Paul, if we realize we are only creating a backdrop for God's message. Life is too short to live petty, broke, and jealous. Everything is about being whole for Christ. Whether in prison, poverty, with riches or without, He speaks to us. For this reason, we are able to step up into the leading role of speaking life to others. This is what Paul was doing. Now we get to take the Bible live! You were born to live your story. Own it, live it, tell it right from where you stand, and watch God give you opportunities to change the budget, setting, and characters of your life. Today is "Take One" of your new story!

Think Better, Do Better:

- *To brush off jealousy and focus on making your own life story, cut off jealous thoughts as soon as you are experiencing them. Then redirect your mind to what you are grateful for right now.*

- *To live the Bible-life: Rehearse your lines (by reading the Word of God), set your stage (by living life and gaining new experiences and trying new things), and share the love of Jesus Christ (by telling of God's goodness, helping in your community, forgiving others, and sharing your gifts).*

GRACE IS GIVEN, NOT DUE

But he said to me, "My grace is sufficient for you, for my power is made perfect in weakness." Therefore I will boast all the more gladly about my weaknesses, so that Christ's power may rest on me. That is why, for Christ's sake, I delight in weaknesses, in insults, in hardships, in persecutions, in difficulties. For when I am weak, then I am strong. **—2 Corinthians 12:9-10**

There is a really good chance that I could be a wonderful gardener if I took it seriously and gave it a shot. My mom had a beautiful garden when I was a little girl. I helped her maintain her fruits and vegetables for years. Sometimes I volunteered. But most of the time it was because I had to do it. My mom had a food garden, but she also grew plenty of flowers, hedges, and ground cover as well. She would plant ground cover in the back yard and decide the next year that she wanted to move it to the front of our home. We would get up before the sun could beat on our backs, dig up the cover, and walk it down our hill of a driveway to plant it in front of the sunporch. I have to admit that my mom was always right. Whatever we were transferring did look great wherever she decided to place it. She was just brilliant in that way.

I have a great eye for arranging shrubs and flowers as well. I just don't have the patience to learn what each needs to survive. Indoor plants that require easy maintenance are all I can manage these days. I do little to no gardening at all. I often say I grew out of landscaping when I grew out of wearing a size 4 jean, and that was a long time ago. I used to water our houseplants until I could see the water raise the soil. Mom used to say, "By the time you see the water at the top, you've probably flooded the plant and smothered its growth." But I always overflooded the plants so that she and I would see the water and know not to water that one again. To this my mom would say, "I don't have to see the water to know you did it, I trust you to do what I say. And besides, it opens up and grows a little more each time you water it."

Just like all of the plants that I've flooded in my lifetime (really...just a few), we are sometimes too full of ourselves. When we are so self-efficient that we are overflowing with pride, we often stunt our own growth. Paul tells us that God said to him, "My grace is sufficient for you, for my power is made perfect in weakness" (2 Corinthians 12:9). God said this in response to Paul's request to have a thorn removed from his side. God let Paul know that He needed to keep this thorn in its place so that Paul would remain in a vulnerable state. For when we are weak, God is strong. In other words, God doesn't need us to prove anything. He trusts us to do what He says and watches us grow a little more each day because of it. We don't have to flood our lives with anything else. God gives us goodness and mercy as a gift. This is His grace towards us.

Like Paul, we can just allow God to be God. We don't have to wrestle with Him because we feel He hasn't removed the thorn from our side. He knows what is causing you grief. God knows exactly what He is doing. For that reason, Paul says in verse 10 of today's text, "That is why, for Christ's sake, I delight in weaknesses, in insults, in hardships, in persecutions, in difficulties. For when I am weak, then I am strong." God has your side, and your back. He loves you so much that He is asking you to shrink your "know it all" so that He can come in and help. What a mighty

Week 3: PB&J: Petty, Broke & Jealous

God we serve!

He just doesn't stop loving us. He gives us grace in all areas of our lives. He said His grace is sufficient. But He left an open ending. He didn't say His grace is sufficient for those that have at least three positions at church. Or for those who tithe the most. Or for those who sit in the first few pews. He says, "My grace is sufficient," and that covers all of our sins. There's no topping God's grace. He's made a habit of giving it where it is needed, not due. That means all who know and trust Him can receive it. But you have to make room for it. Let Him in your heart. When others see Him working in you, you will receive grace while God gets the glory.

Make It a Habit: God wants to be your all in all. Give everything to Him in prayer. Even your sick thoughts. You can simply tell Him, "Lord, I give my spending to You today. Guide my desires so they align with Yours." Or, "Lord, I am already upset just because I have to go to work today. I feel like I need a break and I do not see the light at the end of the tunnel, but I know You are here with me." You don't have enough strength in your reserve, but your God does. May His grace be with you!

PEACE AT HEART

A heart at peace gives life to the body, but envy rots the bones. —**Proverbs 14:30**

We have heard time and time again that stress kills. A heart that is healthy is not controlled by anger, envy, blame, or pettiness. Comparisons are an accelerant to envy. They help us make up things to worry about. We compare ourselves to other women. We compare ourselves to other moms. We compare ourselves to other people of the same height. Then we say things like, "She and I are the same height; I should be as thin as she is." A comparison like that leads to envy, and that person hasn't done anything to intentionally offend us. Comparisons will tear you apart and cause you to rot from the inside out. Contrasts and resentment are symptoms of an unhealthy heart, and an unhealthy heart fosters an unhealthy body. There is really no time for envy. If wholeness is what you want, know that it takes time to embark upon and travel a healthy life journey.

A healthy heart is fueled by the things of God. In Psalm 14:30, David tells us that, "a heart at peace gives life to the body, but envy rots the bones." If there is no attempt to stop decay, anything that spoils on the inside will eventually die. Know that as you live and work for God through your family, church, and community, you become fueled by these things—the things of God. You can stop envy and decay in its tracks. Whatever you need, even if someone else has it, God will bring it to you. God will place doors in front of you and show you how to open them to receive what is yours. Please understand that eventually, you are going to have to decide whether or not you like your life. You are going to have to decide whether or not you love yourself with or without what the world deems as success. Wake up reminding yourself that God is the best decision maker. As you grow through your transformation with these thoughts, also remember God has the best discernment, and He loves you. If you agree with Him, let Him be Lord of your life; you will gradually love yourself more and more as you understand who you are to Him. He loves your different nose, thin eye lashes, and double chin. Our Heavenly Father is a God of action. Make a move for the better today. Don't compare any part of you to someone else today. If God loves you, you are worth loving. Your life is worth living and your body is worth appreciating. You are His own (Isaiah 43:1)!

Drop the game of comparisons and give your body a chance—a chance to be healthy from the heart of you to the skin of you. The comparison voyage is stressful. We have no peace when we constantly compare our living and accomplishments to those of others. When you feel negative on the inside, make it a habit to replace that feeling with a more positive feeling, simply because you know God wants you to do it. If you think as I used to, you'll believe a little envy sparks your competitive nature and launches you into "beast mode." That may be partially true. Still, in addition to pumping you up, that anger and envy is rotting your bones little by little each day. It's not worth it. Let God-things pump you up. It's a healthy way to keep your body clean and well, free of the rot and decay of envy. Be good to you!

Make It a habit: *I make it a practice to give myself something heart-healthy every weekend. This can be anything that makes me feel like I am creating a positive, peaceful me. Try it! Create, cook, or purchase something that generates peace in your world. It can be a heart-healthy snack or any item that provokes a peaceful mindset. It can be a letter or poem to yourself as well. The point is to remind yourself to be good to you without comparing yourself to others for your own peace of mind. God wants and needs you to be strong! Be creative. Make it happen and make it a habit!*

And we know that in all things God works for the good of those who love him, who have been called according to his purpose. —Romans 8:28

When something tragic or inconceivable occurs, it is not uncommon to say something like, "I can't believe he did that." Or, "I can't understand why she thought that was OK." It's just hard to comprehend why people do what they do sometimes. It's hard enough to try to understand why we do the things we do ourselves. We all have strange tendencies of some kind—some more dangerous than others. Everyone who commits a heinous act may not be a horrible person. It may be exactly the opposite. If we weren't there, or didn't receive the information firsthand, we can never really know what drove a person to do what they did. But this is just step one of our trying to process the horrific. For me, I attempt to justify why someone may have been led to do something indescribable, such as a mass bombing or harming a child. Although I might try to figure out "what happened," and my intentions appear to be innocent, questioning someone's motives for their own actions can be a little presumptuous or "judgy," as my daughters would say. There can be a thin line between comprehension and judgment. If not careful, I can go from giving someone the benefit of the doubt to deciding what their sentencing should be on the spot.

We are all different, with diverse upbringings. Even if we use the Bible as our moral guideline, we often tend to determine right or wrong based on our own beliefs and cultural filters. I find it hard to watch the nightly news most of the time. I simply cannot bear to listen to the overstated details that describe the offenses that occur around the world on a daily basis. Seeing the unimaginable highlighted on a regular basis can definitely make one a little judgy from time to time.

My husband used to tell me that everyone doesn't grow up with parents who stress the importance of loving and helping others. In other words, I shouldn't judge people because they don't love the way I love or forgive the way I forgive. I can't get upset because someone shares their emotions less or more than I do. He also used to tell me that everyone doesn't love with the same convictions. Therefore, we have to learn to understand the standards of others, and accept them as they are. This is what amazes me about Romans 8:28: "And we know that in all things God works for the good of those who love him, who have been called according to his purpose."

God is working for the good of those who love Him and are called according to His purpose. He is working for those who love Him and are called. The Scripture doesn't say God is working on behalf of those that love Him perfectly and answer His call right away. He is working for those that love Him right where they are. We can't beat God's giving or loving. He knows we can only love Him the best way we can. He knows us and still calls us! He knows us and still loves us! Let's think about it. Does your love for someone stay the same, even when their love doesn't match your standards? Do you give your all to someone who only loves you when they feel like it? Or when they need you? Or when no one else is around? God does. He makes sure everything works out for our good without saying we have to love Him "the right way" first.

Life is not a test. God just doesn't work that way. He's not the instructor that puts questions on the test that were never discussed (I can't stand that, by the way). He's a merciful God! Isn't it pleasing to serve a God who doesn't log our sins to use them against us? I'm so grateful our God is not petty! We cannot even come close to His love; for God is love (1 John 4:8). Know that God will work it all out for you because He loves you and you have a purpose. But also know that He loves all His children. If we are going to think more like God, we must be less judgy. Why do we feel like people get away with acts we can't fathom doing ourselves? I mean, sure, some tragedies are really beyond our comprehension. Still, for the most part we use our own standards to judge people, even though we know better. Like it or not, if they love God, and are called according to His purpose, God loves the serial killer, as He does the cheating spouse. So, He works it out for them too. God works according to His will. He knows how to squeeze the best from us all. I don't even want to think about the things I've done that God hasn't held against me. Phew!

Those of us that love the Lord and are called according to His purpose are not here to judge one person against another. We're not here to put one generation above the next. Only God has a habit of being perfect. Humans are going to screw things up sometimes. It's what we do. Just chip away at your purpose today. Do that, and you may fall...but you will not fail.

Make It a Habit: Only God can love you right! Don't be amazed when man can't love you the way you want to be loved. You will never find another perfect love like God's. You may never understand His process. But trust that He's got it all, even your heart; and He is working everything out for your good.

DESIRE VS WHAT YOU DESERVE

The desire of the righteous ends only in good, but the hope of the wicked only in wrath. — Proverbs 11:23

How often do we work without the end in mind? I mean, generally speaking, we create something with a result in mind. Whether it's a chair, a house, a story, a work of art, or a program for the local community, we usually form something to use it. Sometimes it's just to admire what we've created. Whatever the endeavor, we usually move dreams from ideas to projects to receive an outcome. We typically have an end in mind. When we work hard on our ventures, we generally want what it is we believe we deserve. This could be anything from compensation to love and respect. It's only human to give and expect something in return.

In Proverbs 11:23, Solomon lets us know that the desire of the righteous ends only in good. This is pretty straightforward. For those who love the Lord, our "strong wants" end well. Our lives down here on earth will end well. But Psalm 37 verse 4 also tells us to take delight in the Lord and He will give the desires of our heart. Simply put, if we live for God, He will give us the desires of our heart. Sometimes, the outcome we believe we deserve, and what we desire, do not line up. For instance, when participating in a disagreement with a spouse or significant other about what's lacking in your relationship, emotions can get high and the situation intense. This is often because each individual wants to be heard and genuinely believes that their perspective is correct. If things escalate, an argument may ensue, and each person eventually wants the other to know that they themselves have won this fight. But winning an argument only satisfies what we believe we deserve at the time. Once we are offended in a discussion, we often end up fighting for the respect we deserve, not the desire to receive what's lacking in the relationship, as we initially stated. Sure, we may have won the battle by proving we can raise our voice as loud as our partner, but no one wins the war.

Everyone should be respected, of course. It's when we focus on that respect and what we deserve, we lose sight of what we desire. We lose sight of the real goal, which is to participate in a gratifying relationship by adding what we believe is really missing. What most of us really desire is to strengthen our unions or relationships. Winning an argument is a small temporary gain. Whether romantic, friendly, parental, or professional, we want the relationship we've invested in to be good. When you are trying to improve a bond, speaking with love instead of harmful comebacks can help you get the results you desire. Why say something harsh? That will only change the direction of the conversation away from what you really want to a battle of respect and self-gain. God doesn't focus on what we deserve. He knows we would all be in trouble. Think bigger, like God. Focus on your desires, your strong wants that will change your life and the lives of those around you. Such things God says will end only in good.

Think Better, Do Better: *There will always be comments or actions that will throw us off our game plan for righteousness. Despite what happens today, put more emphasis on what you desire, not just what you deserve. Whether it's tranquility, productivity, or a full night's rest, whatever your mission, don't get sidetracked. Think on your latter so that it will be greater!*

DROP IT!

Brothers and sisters, I do not consider myself yet to have taken hold of it. But one thing I do: Forgetting what is behind and straining toward what is ahead, I press on toward the goal to win the prize for which God has called me heavenward in Christ Jesus. —Philippians 3:13-14

Occasionally we need to let go. But letting go can be so difficult. Releasing the things that have become a routine part of our lives is trying. Letting go of some of the people from our past is even more difficult. Still, it is extremely necessary. Sometimes the objects from our past can stick to our lives like two-sided tape. When both sticky sides are exposed at the same time, as opposed to preparing one surface at a time, you have trouble getting the tape off of your fingers. The more you touch the tape, the more it keeps sticking to your hands and not the surface for which it was intended. When we try to explain to others why we haven't gotten over a bad habit or old relationship, we sometimes describe it as complicated, or a sticky situation. The more we keep going back to a person and or situation that has tangled us up in a sticky or tricky position, the more difficult it is to get away. That old affiliation may have been good for a while. But to go back to it would be silly since you are not the same person you were when the relationship began. It is so easy to become stuck to a pattern. Maybe that's why Paul thought it was so crucial to speak of moving on in the book of Philippians.

In Philippians 3:13-14, Paul talks about one thing that he hasn't taken hold of yet, but tries to do in order to move forward with his goal through Christ Jesus. Paul states he does one thing, but also adds another. Let's go back to the Scripture. In verse 13, Paul says "Brothers and sisters, I do not consider myself yet to have taken hold of it. But one thing I do..." Then, in verse 14, he says, "Forgetting what is behind and straining toward what is ahead..." He mentions two actions, yet calls them one. This could easily mean nothing if it were written by someone else. But Paul, however, is a very detailed author of the New Testament. After much study, it seems to me that Paul was more than likely stressing here the idea that neither of these actions can be successful without the other. You cannot progress forward without letting go of the past, and you cannot let go of the past without moving forward. The two go hand in hand. If we are going to move forward to thinking more like God, we will have to let go of some deeply rooted habits, childish thoughts, and old relationships. In order to do better, we have to think better. The best habits to create are those of God. If the Bible tells us that we must let go to move forward, and to move forward we must let go, then so be it.

Sometimes we find it difficult to release a particular relationship, because the only common ground is the habit you share. For instance, you may be convicted about gossiping. But you realize the only thing you have in common with your friend is gossiping. You really do nothing else together. Now your new way of thinking is causing you to be convicted when you are with this person. Do you feel led to cut off every relationship with someone who spreads rumors? Not necessarily. Some relationships like this will need your new godly habits and influence. Still, if the person for whom you feel an overwhelming conviction about being around is not willing to stop dragging you into mean conversations and hurtful situations after you've mentioned your new way of thinking, prayer is needed to decide if the relationship needs to continue in the same direction. This will help you understand whether or not the connection needs to change and then continue, or if the relationship needs to be completely disconnected. Either way, your love remains the same for that person.

Throughout our shortfalls God still loves us who love Him. We ought to give the same grace to others. Love completely, pray, and if letting go is necessary...then move on. If moving on is necessary, God will give you instructions to cut off the relationship in love. For example, you may still be with your friend every once in a while, if they agree that gossiping will not be the topic of the day in the future. You may also suggest alternative things to do aside from your normal chatter. Change the topic when you are with this friend. Many of us have thought about doing this, but I'm talking about actually standing for God and going through with it. Chances are, if you continue to be positive and uplifting, your friend will be more uncomfortable around you than you are around them. Either they will change with you or become distant themselves. If they back away, continue to pray for the person. But do move forward. You might have 99 problems, but this doesn't have to be one.

Make It a Habit: If you feel bad, no longer have fun, or dread doing a particular action, you do not have to keep doing it for tradition's sake, or to keep someone else comfortable. Paul said he didn't have it down pat yet, but he was moving forward for God's sake. In other words, he kept trying. He didn't even have the internet. Educate yourself on the best ways to let go if you must. You can find steps to do everything online. Release and press forward. Make it a habit!

WEEK 4:

Think Better, Do Better

BYE-BYE NEGATIVITY

We demolish arguments and every pretension that sets itself up against the knowledge of God, and we take captive every thought to make it obedient to Christ. —2 Corinthians 10:5

Recognition for one of my favorite quotes has been given to several people over the years. Lena Horne is one who has been given credit for stating, "It's not the load that breaks you down; it's the way you carry it." I'm not sure who coined the phrase, but it really hits home for me. One of the toughest circumstances for me to recover from is the loss of a loved one. When I was 20 years old, my fiancé and I set our wedding date for September 14, 1991. Two weeks before our wedding date however, my mother suddenly passed away in her sleep. We had her home-going service on September 7, and we got married as planned the following Saturday. I was devastated. My mother had been instrumental in the planning of my entire wedding. Not to mention the fact that we went everywhere together. I am the only girl and the youngest of three children in my family. It was nothing for my mom and I to do something together every weekend. When the first responders stated they were still trying, but my mom wasn't responding to their efforts to revive her, I felt like someone had literally pulled the rug from under my feet and placed a table on my chest. I walked to the nearest window, stared at the sky, and asked God,

> *"Now what? I know You didn't allow me to give my life to you to be torn down by this. I still trust You, and I am not OK right now. I know I may be, in maybe five or ten years from now. But right now, I am lost, Jesus, and I need You to tell me what to do."*

God is so faithful. I plainly heard a voice say, Look around the room. So I did. I quickly noticed my dad was lost and needed me. So I started there. Then I watched my mom's body bounce up and down off of the stretcher as the paramedics continued to use the defibrillator in the ambulance on the way to the hospital. I remember thinking such thoughts as "Would God let you give your life to Him and then snatch your mom from you like this? You only recently learned to trust Him. Is God even real? This doesn't make sense." I cried and started praying again in the ambulance,

> *"I am losing it, Lord. I will be the only one at the hospital for a while, and I am slowly losing it right now. I know I'm going to break down because I'm human, but help my mind so that I can handle this and be the daughter she raised me to be throughout this whole ordeal. I just want to get it together and be a blessing for You. I am 20 years old and You know I don't know what to do next. You are going to have to hold me together because I can't.*

He did. I got out of the vehicle and handled business. When all of our family showed up, my aunties took over, and I began to mourn. It was terrible. But every once in a while I couldn't help but smile because I remembered two things:

> *1.) My mom had revealed to me for the first time, the night before, that she'd had a relationship with God and that it was better than I ever knew. She explained that she didn't always speak it like I did or show it as I chose to do. Glory!*

2.) I was about to faint in the ambulance because I was traumatized. Still, God showed up and helped me change my thoughts just because I asked and chose to believe, even after doubt! I literally had to keep giving praise to God while at the hospital.

Paul said, "We demolish arguments and every pretension that sets itself up against the knowledge of God, and we take captive every thought to make it obedient to Christ (2 Corinthians 10:5). In this text, Paul was telling the people of Corinth that as Christians, we fight against principalities and spirits. We fight a little differently than the world does. By saying we take captive every thought to make it obedient to Christ, Paul let us know that we will have thoughts that don't line up with God's Word. Still, we can take those same thoughts captive. Paul says we can change these thoughts. We don't have to wait to think differently. Since God allowed me to change my most traumatic thoughts, I am able to use this victory against my flesh and the enemy when I am sick and I hear a voice say, "Your family could progress much better without having to take care of you all the time. It would be so much better for them if you weren't' here. You are weak; that's why you are not healed yet." If you have ever had thoughts remotely similar to these, please remember, the devil is the best liar. We often joke when we say it, but it's true. Don't let his influence denounce what God says about you.

Negative thoughts will flood your mind occasionally. But you can take those same thoughts and change them in the way that Paul mentioned. Grab those thoughts and make those thoughts obedient to your God! I sometimes stop harmful thoughts of myself right in the middle and say out loud, "This is not me; that is not true!" Then I actually replace the thought by putting something else on my mind. That's it. If you entertain destructive thinking, it will smother your determination like mold on a damp basement wall. My friend, train your mind. Think on what is positive at the time. Sometimes, the destructive thoughts keep coming. That's fine, just keep capturing them and pushing them off to God. Just as He did for me, He will strengthen your mind and your heart.

Make It a Habit: The devil is good at sending us negative thoughts that appear logical. Don't justify them. When it comes to loss, having sorrowful thoughts is standard. Our loved ones are worth our tears. But pity for ourselves is unproductive. It's tough, but you can carry the torch for your loved one from here. This is the one time bullying is OK. Day by day, stiff arm the enemy, look past his games, and keep going, knowing you are filled with God's power. For more encouragement, look to Ephesians 1:19-21. Keep fighting. God is with you!

THE REAL FAKE NEWS

DAY
23

For the Spirit God gave us does not make us timid, but gives us power, love and self-discipline. —2 Timothy 1:7

Home alone one evening, I heard a low thud come from the second floor. A few minutes later, I heard another thump. My dog and I were still on the first floor. I didn't panic after the first sound because our house is old, and you tend to hear a thing or two when it's quiet. Besides, my dog didn't respond. Neither of us are concerned when it's a sound we've heard before. The second time we heard a thud, the dog and I both took careful notice. His ears raised up and he ran and sat in front of the stairs. All types of scenarios ran through my mind. I became a fully trained ninja in my head within seconds. I waited another minute. Then I heard the rain start coming through the bathroom window into my bathroom. It was just the wind. When I went upstairs, I found that the wind was blowing so hard, it knocked down the shampoo and conditioner bottles that were left in the windowsill. The storm had caused such noises before. I knew this. I usually go right back to whatever I'm doing without fear. This time, for some reason, was different. Even after I knew the wind was the culprit, I had this paralyzing fear in my body that kept me in the same room the entire evening. It was strange.

We create the best stories in our own mind. If we consider the fact that no one was in my home to harm me, nothing was there to physically keep me from getting a glass of water in the kitchen. Nothing was blocking me from having a great quiet evening except my own collection of "what ifs" in my own head. What if someone is here? What if someone has been here all day? Morbid ideas kept me restrained to one room. Really? One room...all evening? Before I knew it, my family was home from living their daily lives and I had never left the room.

Paul states in 2 Timothy 1:7, "For the Spirit God gave us does not make us timid, but gives us power, love and self-discipline." Have you ever had a great idea for a blog, book, business, or invention, and talked yourself out of it just as quickly as the entrepreneurial thought appeared in your brain? Does the notion of creating or building something on your own bring tightness straight to your stomach? It has for me, many...many times. It still does. As I pray and prepare myself each time I sit down to write, I pray that God will take away everything that is not of Him, that I might be used for His glory. For one, we are nothing without God's guidance; but also, any fear that is present usually comes from the list of "what ifs" I've created in my own head.

It's not that fear is so powerful. It is our attention to fear that make it so powerful. If we don't lend fear our respect, it has nothing. Every party we have with fear is a BYOT (Bring Your Own Thoughts) affair. If you don't bring the "what ifs" to the table, there is no fear at all. Our beliefs are so powerful that they can make the most unrealistic dangers seem real. We can sit in a crowded movie theatre and project the same feelings of being alone as the girl running through the dark woods on the screen. Her fears become our fears because our bodies can't tell the difference between faux harm and actual danger. Our senses respond in the same way. We often tense up tight to the core, eyes wide open, and ears on alert in movie theaters. Some viewers scream when the characters scream and enjoy being frightened in this manner. The point is, we respect this type of fear and let it in for the sake of entertainment. In real life, we respect fear since it can help us prepare for the "what ifs" and keep us safe—the "what ifs" that make us close the blinds and walk each other to our cars at night. We don't often realize fright keeps us from the prospering "what ifs." What if I try and win?" What if I learn something new?

We have no business holding on to fear. The Bible says those of us that follow Christ were not given it. According to 2 Timothy 1:7, fear is not a part of our inheritance. God didn't pass it down to us. Understand, this means we get it elsewhere and are passing it down and around to our family and friends. We project our fears onto our children if we're not careful. We make it heritable. Fear comes in many shapes, sizes, and phrases: "Why do you want to do that? Aren't you afraid of people knowing so much about you?" "What if it doesn't work; then what?" "I would be so scared if I were you."

Ladies, God did not make us to live timidly! We honor God, we give Him lordship over our lives. Therefore, the one healthy fear is the reverence that lives because we acknowledge Him. It causes us to walk with confidence; not stop in terror. It causes us to take precautions and keep charging! The alarm you sense before crossing the street that causes you to look both ways...yes, keep that awareness. But God doesn't give us a fear of progressing, changing, trailblazing, or simply living. If He didn't create us to live with a spirit of fear, that means we are not created to live in it. Sure, fear can and will be present. But the power that our Scripture speaks of is discharged as you jump over your fears. Jump past them. Visually grab God's hand and jump. If you are already existing for God, your desires will be lined up with His and the discipline of ignoring this type of fear will come.

Make It a Habit: Each time you conquer fear, share with others how you did it. Pass down encouragement, not trepidation. This, my friend, is how we end transmissible or heritable fear. Press on and enjoy your journey!

WHAT'S UPSTAIRS AND NOTHING ELSE

Finally, brothers and sisters, whatever is true, whatever is noble, whatever is right, whatever is pure, whatever is lovely, whatever is admirable—if anything is excellent or praiseworthy—think about such things. —Philippians 4:8

When you are not where you should be in life, it takes great awareness of yourself and others to stop and get refocused. Some individuals just have the natural ability to buckle down and adapt. Others learn a way to make it happen and own it. The idea that we can calm ourselves to a place where intellect and discernment take over so that we can adapt to our surroundings is simply remarkable to me. People use many different tactics to stay calm and focused when stakes are high. Wellness professionals suggest breathing techniques, stretching exercises, tension release drills, and music breaks to name a few. Serena Williams once told Sports Illustrated that she wins most of her Grand Slams because of what's upstairs and nothing else. She said that when she's behind, that's when she relaxes the most. She just slows down and focuses on one point at a time [1].

Having a few moments to decide how to handle a serious situation can be overwhelming. Thinking of whether or not to have surgery, testing alternative medications, deciding if a family member should stay on life support or to allow the doctors to remove the breathing apparatus. These choices can shake up your life. Sometimes it is not even the short timespan or a life-and-death condition that adds the heaviness to our circumstances. It may just be the everyday contexts of life all by itself. Deciding which bill to pay immediately—how much to pay on this one or that one. Decisions of how to help loved ones without squeezing your own bank account. Making the choice of whether or not to further your education and increase student loans. Any of the before-mentioned conditions have the propensity to cause havoc at the moment they are dropped in your lap. But the truth of the matter is, we have a choice. Game-changer decisions have the tendency to make us forget we have a choice in the matter at hand. We can get so wrapped up in the severity of the issue that we can lose control and sight of our goal.

Paul writes to his brothers and sisters in Philippi to urge them to stand firm in the Lord. He ultimately says to them, "Finally, brothers and sisters, whatever is true, whatever is noble, whatever is right, whatever is pure, whatever is lovely, whatever is admirable—if anything is excellent or praiseworthy—think about such things" (Philippians 4:8). "Think on these things," he says. When you are trying to come to a decision, think of what is right, think of not just your immediate needs. Serena Williams said she just focuses on the point at hand. She makes the best moves without freaking out over what will happen next. When I'm in a tough spot, especially when I'm angry, I try to think of the move I need to make right now that will represent God the best. To be completely transparent, this idea may be second to a few not-so-godly words that go through my mind first. However, thinking of what is pure, right, and praiseworthy helps me know that the actions I am about to take will not reflect poorly on the Kingdom of God. I try to take them one step at a time. Now, I definitely get tired of taking the high road, or being the one to remain centered in some instances. I often want to go off script every once in a while. However, too much is at stake. Particularly if God has called you to be a leader. I'm sure I'm not the only one who is tired of being in the same situation over and over again. I'm not saying we always create these sets of tired circumstances that keep arising to strum our nerves. Sometimes it is just the environment of doing ministry and church itself (Lord, have mercy!). Tough choices must be made.

I often have to remind myself not to let the number of times I'm in a situation, or the cruelty of the matter, organize my steps when I'm in a crunch. Don't let anger or panic take you away from righteous views. We have to make vigilant choices as children of God. We cannot become reckless just because the stakes have gotten so high. If we are going to walk around declaring God is our everything, then He should be worthy of our careful decision making. Calm down, breathe, stay alert, and think on the things that are pure and right. No matter how heavy the load, you've got this! Remember how it feels to make the right moves. Remember the peace you received from doing so. Then when it's crunch time and another big choice needs to be made, imagine the peace to come, and think on these things!

Make It a Habit: *When you are at the place where you need to make a game-changer decision, think of Moses, who had to go back to Egypt, from which he fled as a felon, to set his people free. Think positively and courageously. Don't just go through the motions. Be intentional. Fill your mind with praise songs, Scriptures, and hymns that the Holy Spirit can bring back to your remembrance on days like this. God didn't let His Son die on the cross so that we might die. He did so that we might live! Refocus point by point today. Today's match is yours!*

---

[1] Livni, Ephrat. "A tip from Serena Williams can help you win in everyday life." Quartz. 2018. https://qz.com/1319629/a-tip-from-serena-williams-can-help-you-win-in-everyday-life/

WINNING IN OVERTIME

"For I know the plans I have for you," declares the Lord, "plans to prosper you and not to harm you, plans to give you hope and a future." —Jeremiah 29:11

It's been said that when you are starting to work yourself thin, you are no longer working on purpose; you're working on passion. To be frank, during my first hearing of this, I wasn't quite sure the latter was so bad. I mean, after all, passion is fuel, hunger, desire...right? It's what keeps us persistently driving frontward. Honestly, I don't believe functioning with passion in mind is so terrible. However, I do understand how working on passion alone is dangerous, which is what I believe may have been the firm basis of the author's intent.

At one point, the people of Israel were in exile from Jerusalem to Babylon. Hananiah, a dishonest prophet, had given the people of Israel false hope by stating that God was going to break the hold of Nebuchadnezzar on all nations within two years.

Week 4: Think Better, Do Better

Jeremiah told Hananiah God's plan to let Hananiah die within two years for speaking false prophecies to the people of Israel (Jeremiah 28:10-16). In Jeremiah 29, verses 4-14, Jeremiah wrote to the surviving elders, priests, and all others Nebuchadnezzar sent astray. Jeremiah gave the people a true message from God. He told them to build houses, settle down, plant gardens, marry, and not decrease in number. God also told the people through Jeremiah that He would bring them back from exile after 70 years. Yes, this is right. God said the people will come back from exile after 70 years. We sometimes miss the fact that this is the information given to the people of Israel, mostly because it was written right before the revealing of a well-known verse we often quote as Christians: "'For I know the plans I have for you,' declares the Lord, 'plans to prosper you and not to harm you, plans to give you hope and a future'" (Jeremiah 29:11).

Before the Israelites were told that God's plan was to prosper them, they learned this thriving would not physically take place for 70 more years. In other words, not only would some of the Israelites be gone from earth when this prophecy came to fruition; they also had to endure right then knowing the situation was more than likely not going to change in their lifetime. They had to withstand their circumstances while knowing only the next generations would live better.

Tilling the land, rearing children, and building a place to stay where you don't want to be had to be so difficult at times for the Israelites. Life dynamics are never simple. One of the toughest jobs in the world in my mind is being a single parent. Single parents often take care of several conditions on a daily basis so that their children will not feel a gap in love or care. I imagine this job to be even more challenging for those who do it on passion alone, without a sense of purpose from God. Why? Well, if passion is our fuel, it will eventually run out at one point or another, which leads to burnout and exhaustion. It can cause feelings of ineffectiveness and lack of accomplishment.

But purpose from God allows us to work hard while yet being tired. Laboring with your end in mind, knowing why you must persevere, gives one a sense of hope and drive to make it through—even if your location or state of being doesn't change, like the Israelites'. Knowing what you do now will not go in vain, because the next generation will reap the benefits, is at least something to work towards. It gives us purpose. God is a just God and a loving God. Our future is good! God may allow trouble to last all night. But know that joy is coming! He knows the plans He has for us. Yes, He wants the best for us. He wants us to live well. He came that we might have life, and life more abundantly (John 10:10). Stand on His promises while you grind. Believe what He says. When you feel like all you do is work, hold on, hold on, hold on! Hold on and look to God! Ask Him to help increase your faith. Keep building; keep planting seeds of the gospel wherever you go. Tell of His faithfulness. This is a part of our purpose. You cannot give up. Just because you've been working hard and long doesn't mean God doesn't care and you're not coming out. This too shall pass. You are coming out of this, but it must be His way. Since Jesus died for our sins, it doesn't matter what the game is, we win! Your situation seems like a game in overtime. I get it. Keep digging. Keep grinding. It doesn't matter how long; just stay woke! God is for us and He is with us. Please hang in there. Hold on. In the end, we win!

Make It a Habit: *God has a plan. If you're having trouble seeing the light at the end of the tunnel right now, ask God for a faith exchange. Give him your will for His way by being patient and trusting him. You can seek wise counsel from someone you trust as well. Keep in mind, the same God that put the stars in the sky is looking out for you and longing to carry you through. Hold on, my sister, hold on!*

JUMP!

Trust in the Lord with all your heart and lean not on your own understanding; in all your ways submit to him, and he will make your paths straight. **—Proverbs 3:5-6**

It seems the older we get the fewer people we trust. My husband and I used to laugh and say we couldn't wait to grow old together so that we could be two of the older saints who trust no one and give everyone "a piece of their mind" without fear of repercussion. Apparently, that time is sneaking up on me way sooner than I thought. I have not gotten to the place where I want to tell everyone what I'm thinking about them or their actions. However, I do find myself trusting the same few people for everything without any confidence in others. The fact that I'm an extreme introvert doesn't help. Introverts are energized by having time alone. This often keeps me from reaching out to new individuals, which makes it easier to lean on my own understanding. We can receive so much wisdom from friends and persons who know us or have experienced what we're going through. We can ask for help and avoid suffering alone. Still, we often trust no one and lean on our own understanding.

The book of Proverbs is known to contain the wisdom of life. Its very purpose is to give knowledge of wisdom and instruction. Solomon (son of David) says in Proverbs 3:5-6, "Trust in the Lord with all your heart and lean not on your own understanding; in all your ways submit to Him, and He will make your paths straight." These words come to us as direction born from a place of righteousness and experience. Solomon encourages virtuous living through practical means. He tells us how to live under God's direction with a hands-on approach. He simply passes down insight to his next generation in this message. It is very clear. Solomon basically states, "Trust God, not yourself."

When we lean on our own rationale, we are prone to take less chances. We tend to stay comfortable and play it safe. I woke up one morning from a dream that left me excited and eager to break through my ceiling of comfort. I woke up ready for adventure. I had a dream that my immediate family and I were in the sky, hopping from cloud to cloud. Each member of my family was smiling, skipping from one big cloud to another bigger cloud. They each were encouraging me to leap as well. I finally got up the nerve to jump. I bent my knees and went to take off, and I couldn't move. Right before I went to lift my body, I noticed that I could fall if I didn't clear the landing, and therefore never moved. I realized falling meant I could possibly die; therefore, I froze. I tried to jump once more. I prepared to take off and woke up wanting to go back to my dream so I could be fulfilled like the rest of my family. I told my husband and children about the dream, and everyone said the same thing: "Sounds like you need to do what you would tell us to do: leap! You woke up in time to hop to the next level in real life, in time to do whatever it is God is pressing on your heart." Now here I sit, writing as I knew the Lord called me to do.

Following God, trusting the Word, and not leaning on your own understanding of life alone can be tricky if you just keep listening to sermons, going to Bible studies, reading devotionals, and never changing anything. God is calling each of us to something. You may feel led to volunteer for community efforts. Maybe you want to help the sick by making meals and delivering them from your home. You may sense the need to start a Bible lesson or to create a conference for a certain group of people. Whatever God is calling you to do, reach for it! Seek wisdom on the subject and go for it. No one can pull your feet off the cloud you stand on now. You must buckle down, prepare for the launch. We often wonder why we are so unsatisfied. We don't know where the inner lack of fulfillment comes from. It can easily come from the emptiness we feel when we are not doing what we sense we should be doing. When we have a calling we're ignoring, there is often a dark hole in our being that can only be filled by stepping out on faith. You are fearfully and wonderfully made (Psalm 139:14). Use what you got, to get what you want.

Make It a Habit: Years ago, I heard that when we find ourselves annoyed, angry, unfulfilled, and discouraged, it is usually because we are not giving to others. You are just bubbling over with substance to share. You do not have to sit filled to the rim with purpose. Pour out some of what God is giving you so that others can gain wisdom to fulfill their purpose too. You more than likely know what it is you need to do. If you don't, pray and seek the wisdom of someone you trust. They can often help you put pieces together that you didn't know connected. Trust me, it may not be easy. But the joy of just working towards the goal you are to reach is so satisfying. The more you do it each day, or week, the more of a habit it becomes. Just do it until it becomes a habit!

THE STRUGGLE IS REAL

We know that the law is spiritual; but I am unspiritual, sold as a slave to sin. I do not understand what I do. For what I want to do I do not do, but what I hate I do. And if I do what I do not want to do, I agree that the law is good. As it is, it is no longer I myself who do it, but it is sin living in me. For I know that good itself does not dwell in me, that is, in my sinful nature. For I have the desire to do what is good, but I cannot carry it out. For I do not do the good I want to do, but the evil I do not want to do—this I keep on doing. Now if I do what I do not want to do, it is no longer I who do it, but it is sin living in me that does it.

So I find this law at work: Although I want to do good, evil is right there with me. For in my inner being I delight in God's law; but I see another law at work in me, waging war against the law of my mind and making me a prisoner of the law of sin at work within me. What a wretched man I am! Who will rescue me from this body that is subject to death? Thanks be to God, who delivers me through Jesus

Christ our Lord! So then, I myself in my mind am a slave to God's law, but in my sinful nature a slave to the law of sin. **—Romans 7:14-25**

I completed my college degree after I was married with children. I attended a program where all class updates on your research had to be given in the form of a presentation to later be included as a part of your own written published work. I recall thinking about the instructor, "Oh my goodness, Sir, you absolutely hate me!" I didn't mind speaking publicly too much. It was the fact that the presentations were precisely timed. This made me nervous. When nervous, or just thinking deeply, I had the tendency to say "um" out loud. I also needed to speak loudly and clearly so that the entire room could hear me. Ugh...I totally hated it! Well, the first few presentations were painful. I had to intentionally pause in order to suppress my ums. I must say, I was told I did an excellent job each time. Still, I did not like going through the process at all. I did however recognize the fact that a change had to be made within me. I had a habit to break. I knew this would be a great help to me in the future. Yet, I loathed every time I had to present, and loved each time it was over. When all was said and done, I felt accomplished. I still say um once in a while when speaking publicly, but not nearly as much as before the class. Some habits are hard to break.

Repeating words over and over or smoking a cigarette when nervous are just behaviors people do without even realizing it. We can make such actions with absolutely no thought. This is what makes them so hard to change. We can describe some sin this way. We do it automatically. In Romans 7:14-25, Paul tells us of his personal struggle with sin. Since we usually see Paul's faith expressed so confidently, many theologians have different opinions on whether or not he was speaking about his past or current struggles with evil. Since Romans 7:14-25 was written in the present tense, several experts believe his struggles were current. For the purpose of this idea, I'll do the same.

Paul uses many words that suggest his current situation was the topic of his discussion. The language can be difficult to understand, but Paul simply creates a few themes in Romans 7:14-25:

Week 4: Think Better, Do Better

- *I am aware of my sinful nature.*

- *I know what is right and I want to do it most of the time, but can't.*

- *There is a war of sin going on within me.*

- *Thanks be to God, who delivers me through Jesus Christ our Lord!*

I love that Paul, with all his accomplishments, admits that he is a slave to sin without Christ. We are able to read of a powerful apostle who is really like us. It is comforting to know that Paul knew what was right and kept doing wrong too. Hello—story of my life! One moment I'm on top of the world because I feel like I'm doing God's will. The next moment my thoughts and actions cause me to wonder if I'm really a child of God. Thankfully, Paul reminds us that this view is typical through Romans chapter 7. We battle with right and wrong because we are human. It is part of our nature. None of us is holy and sin-free (see also Romans 3:22-24).

But just like Paul, we cannot do it alone. We have to spend time with God to fight back. We need His love to forgive ourselves and try again. Sadly, guilt is destructive. It makes drawing near to God difficult when we are ashamed. I often have the attention span of a gnat, especially when I feel guilty. My prayer can be spontaneous and all over the place. This is why it is so great that things change when we call His name. Sometimes I just call on the name of Jesus and feel the strength of Him behind me. Before my situation even changes, my mindset is altered because I remember the victories of my past when I call on Christ Jesus. I stand up on the inside like my daddy just showed up with a new bike in front of the kids that bragged about getting theirs first. It's a wrap!

Don't feel bad that you know you're are a sinful mess without God. Know that you are nothing without Him! This is why He is with us. Knowing who you are without God helps you remember who you are because of Him! We don't just want God; we need God. There's a sure enough sin war going on in each of us, and grace is on our side. Even Paul knew what was right and couldn't do it all the time. God still allowed Paul's words to be included in the Bible as part of our instructions for living. He states, "Thanks be to God, who delivers me through Jesus Christ our Lord!" (Romans 7:25). Yes, he said, "delivers"—as in, God continues to deliver me through Jesus Christ. God continues to deliver you because He knows you are not always capable of doing the right you want to do. No one is able to be sinless. Keep your head up like Paul. He was aware of his sinful nature. Don't hide from God. He wants to hear from you as you are.

Make It a Habit: *Make it a habit to go to God no matter what. Make it a habit to call on Him anytime. When you don't know what to say, just start calling His name. As you do, know that God is an active listener. He hears you and responds!*

DON'T WASTE YOUR TIME

Therefore, there is now no condemnation for those who are in Christ Jesus. —Romans 8:1

Plain and simple, Paul moves from the topic of sin in Romans chapter 7 to victory over it in Romans 8. In Romans 8:1, he says, "There is now no condemnation for those who are in Christ Jesus." He lets us know God doesn't condemn us as Satan would have us think. Paul throws a wrench in Satan's web of deceptions. Deceptions of embarrassment and humiliation. We sometimes have no problem sliding past our moral boundaries when in a group. This is when we tend to ignore our moral compass and go with the flow like everyone else. While the crowd is still near, our sins feel like small transgressions that managed to get a little out of hand. Later, a subtle dose of mortification shows up when we're by ourselves. The disgrace of wrongdoings creeps up on us and keeps us company when we are alone and vulnerable. Once they're settled in, we begin to play a lonely game of Shame on Me. Condemnation now seems warranted and we punish ourselves over and over. Paul thinks differently.

In Genesis 3:8-19, God speaks to Adam about not answering when God called him. Adam's excuse was that he was naked and didn't want God to see him. God asked Adam how Adam was aware of his nakedness, and asked if he'd eaten from the tree of the knowledge of good and evil as he was instructed not to do. Adam admitted the woman God created for him gave him the fruit of the tree. The woman confessed she took fruit as the serpent suggested. This is when man learned he was flawed and covered up his sins. The serpent, the man, and the woman participated in wicked conduct. Still, instead of answering God and confessing wrong took place, Adam and Eve took on shame. Eventually, each party paid the price of their sins. (Please read Genesis 3:8-19 for the consequences this team paid for their sins, which took place before Christ's birth, death, and resurrection.) Because of Christ, the sins of those who believe in Him are handled differently now. Instead of death, we have forgiveness! This is why Paul says in Romans 8:1, "There is therefore now no condemnation for those who are in Christ Jesus."

What a gracious God we serve! We are free from the law of sin and death. God does not want us to spend time beating ourselves up over sin. Don't waste your energy. You can put that same time and vitality into learning how to do better. We see what good sulking did for the first man and woman God created.

Hear what the Lord is saying and do not condemn yourself. You won't get extra points for feeling terrible about yourself. God is not like us. He is not waiting with a switch in Heaven for your next punishment. He knows your mind, soul, body, and spirit. He is waiting to pour His love on you like maple syrup on a stack of pancakes. God made a way for us to be forgiven. Yes, Christ died for us to be able to pick up and keep it moving. This is cause for worship, not shame. Confess your sin to God. He will forgive. Follow His lead and do the same (see also 1 John 1:7-9).

Make It a Habit:

Don't:

- *Let the embarrassment of sin keep you down.*

- *Don't give up growing wherever you can.*

- *Don't let the enemy tell you God is upset with you.*

Do:

- *Get right back on the wagon. Whether it's living a simpler life to give more to others, ditching complaining, letting go of a romantic relationship that is filling your time but draining your soul, or forsaking the ever-so-tempting gossip, just keep trying so that the evil fails and God gets the glory! He loves you!*

MODEL BEE-HAVIOR

For you created my inmost being; you knit me together in my mother's womb. I praise you because I am fearfully and wonderfully made; your works are wonderful; I know that full well. —Psalm 139:13-14

When my mother passed away, I was 20 years old. After her passing, I did not understand how you could meet me and know the real me. I felt as though all who met me after my mom was gone would never meet the real Tamara. The me that smiled all the time, worked out all the time, and enjoyed life no matter what. I knew God was working something through me at that time. Still, I felt my mom being in reach made me so much better.

My mom and dad fought like cats and dogs yet still loved each other as if they were the last two people on earth. We didn't go to church every Sunday, but my mom pushed me all the time to do what was right. She never let someone go without if she had what they needed. I mean never. Although impressively gorgeous and humble, she always taught us that no one cares what you look like if you're ugly on the inside. I wanted to be just like her. So when the time came for the viewing of the body, I dressed myself as my mom taught me for such an occasion and stood at the end of the casket so that everyone could see her life continue through me.

My mom died suddenly at 51, so I wanted people to see in me a little bit of what she created while she was here. My brothers Mike and Fred agreed. The next few months without her were absolutely horrible. My family missed her tremendously and I was mystified. My husband recorded a message on our voicemail system as our alarm clock so that I would hear a portion of Proverbs 139 each morning. It encouraged me and gave me the desire to get out of bed. Psalm 139:13-14 reads: "For you created my inmost being; you knit me together in my mother's womb. I praise you because I am fearfully and wonderfully made; your works are wonderful; I know that full well."

Psalm 139 was my voicemail wake-up call for years, but these two verses stuck out particularly during my time of heartache. Still, I wanted stories and advice from my mom on how to raise my girls. As mentioned earlier, my mom didn't take us to church very often. However, the very night before she passed, she told me that she gave her life to God a long time ago. I was left with that wonderful assurance. Nevertheless, I had begun to receive so much wisdom from my faith community that I couldn't imagine life without constantly attending a worship service. I wondered how my mom, her mother, and my aunties, poured so much godly wisdom and principles into us without the constant fellowship of the church. What did they have down in them that kept them lined up with God? Well, years later I learned this:

One of the ways queen bees become queens is they are fed queen jelly exclusively. All bee larvae are fed some queen jelly, but only the queens are fed queen jelly solely. This allows the queen to develop far beyond the worker bee into the mature female she was created to become. In other words, "Train up a child in the way he should go, and when he is old, he will not depart from it" (Proverbs 22:6). Feed your children what they need to sustain them in this world. Yes, they need the Word of God. They also need examples of the Word. I'm not suggesting you forsake the fellowship of God's people. Our faith community provides us with a unique support system as we worship and develop together. But, quoting Scriptures day and night means nothing if we don't teach our children how to love, share, give, forgive, and forgive again.

Sometimes I care more about people's success than they do themselves. It's what I know how to do best. Helen Killings, my mother, taught me that. She taught me that I am fearfully and wonderfully made and that everything God makes is beautiful. She used to speak of God when I didn't even know what she was talking about. When she died, my grandmother and aunties taught me to cry, stand up, and keep moving. They told me I would cry all the time and it was fine. Just pray, get up when I could, and rest when my body told me to do so. Get back up when strong, and rest again when necessary. When I couldn't get up, my family stepped in for me. But they always made sure I got back up again. See, these are godly principles. God is a respecter of principles. His Word is filled with values for us to encompass. Many of us know women who fed us the principles of God in order to become virtuous women. This is the stuff we can't forget. Godly principles, that's queen jelly! The Word, that's queen jelly! Love, that's queen jelly! Faith, that's queen jelly! This is the main course.

I'm not sure how my mom felt about us not going to church all of the time. Since she went home to heaven the next morning, I never got a chance to ask. But I do know my mom now wears a crown since she confessed that she believed in God with her whole heart. She understood the principles of God and modeled them in her own way. This is virtuous woman behavior. Let's feed young girls all over the world queen jelly exclusively. Leave the legacy of a godly queen.

Make It a Habit: *Today, remember, you have royalty inside your DNA. Consume yourself with His promises to nourish the queen within, and be sure to nurture another queen-to-be.*

FREEDOM

DAY 30

So if the Son sets you free, you will be free indeed.
—John 8:36

Have you ever had all the facts about a situation, yet still felt something wasn't adding up? Two details plus two more details just didn't equal four? With good intentions, people around you try to ease your discomfort and suspicions, but you know there is more to the equation. Eventually, you receive the missing pieces of the puzzle and you tell yourself you will trust your instincts from now on. Immediately you gain tenacity and courage.

Maybe you were told your professional goals were irrational, irrelevant, or impossible to reach. You find a resource that supports and endorses your ideas and you feel vindicated as though you've been released to exhale and excel. The truth has a way of lifting restraints and gifting liberty. This is what most of us really want—to be free from all that has us bound and enslaved. Whether it is physical, mental,

Week 4: Think Better, Do Better

or spiritual freedom, people just want to be able to live their lives and enjoy the journey. Quite often, relishing the journey has a cost. Some enjoy the thrill of driving a car full-speed down a straightaway, though the action of doing so has the potential to be exhilarating, dangerous, and most likely illegal. If the roads are wet, you may feel exhilarated, but you might also end up in a terrible crash. There are many circumstances that make us feel free for a while. However, the only way to be free forever, or free indeed, is to be freed by Christ.

A serious conversation takes place in John chapter 8. Jesus lets the Pharisees, the religious leaders of the time, know that they may be free from physical slavery, but they weren't free indeed. They did not believe Jesus was Lord because they were listening to their acting father, the devil. This in turn made them partially free. Jesus told those that believed in Him that the only way to be truly free was to be free through Him, Jesus Christ. To be free from bondage and eternal damnation is to live totally unrestricted. Those in the crowd were still slaves. Jesus let the people know that nonbelievers who sin are slaves to sin (John 8:34). Before God enters the picture, the pieces of the puzzle just don't add up.

God's Got a Habit : God's Unconditional Love

He's got a habit of loving us! God knows we can't live freely without Him. The pieces of the puzzle would never come together, and we would never reach our potential. All would be slaves to whatever sins we could unearth. God never stops making a way for us. He gave His Son, who died and rose to give us eternal life instead of eternal damnation for the wrong we've done. Now Christ lives at the right hand of God that we might communicate with Him to gain strength to conquer the sin that keeps us from living healthy and free.

John 8:31-32 states: "To the Jews who had believed him, Jesus said, 'If you hold to my teaching, you are really my disciples. Then you will know the truth, and the truth will set you free.'" Also, Jesus said in John 14:6, "I am the way and the truth and the life. No one comes to the Father except through me."

Putting it all together, if Jesus is the truth, and the truth will set us free, we will know the truth (Jesus) by holding to His teachings. In other words, to know Jesus is to hold on to the Word of God and stay concentrated on the Word of God. That's it, ladies! The only way to be free from the fear of becoming who you really are is to know the truth. The only way

159

to get what God has for you is to know the truth. The only way to defeat the enemy is to know the truth. The only way to step out on faith is to know the truth. The only way to live with no regret and live eternally is to know the truth...the truth about who you are to God, and who He wants to be to you.

Jesus is the truth and the life! Allow Him to help elevate your existence. There is freedom in living for Christ. You're no longer bogged down with popular opinion or ulterior motives. Now you also live by truth. When you tell the truth, there is no other story to tell. Your life will speak for itself. You'll have to get rid of some stuff. To think more like God is to let go of what's not like Him. No more hating your body. No more waiting for more money to live better. No more using social media to determine your next direction. No more ignoring the truth to save a relationship going nowhere. Take off the weight of bad attitudes, shady comments, and "He is mine" fights! Your desire to think like God must trump everything. You will have to be intentional and purposeful or, trust me, you will quit and rely on your own thoughts again. Embrace Jesus as the whole truth to live, think, and love as He does! It can be tough, but He is worth it!

Make It a Habit: Since God has a habit of loving us unconditionally, and we strive to think as He, our love for ourselves and others will be limitless! Our victories... endless! Jealousy, for what? It's irrelevant. You need only compete with yourself to Think Better and Do Better! No one can do, get, achieve, enjoy what God has for you. So forgiveness, we can welcome it. Yes...we welcome forgiveness! Grudges are a waste of time for those that strive to be more like Christ. Let the faults of no man keep you from what God has for you! Live and love freely! You are at liberty to love unconditionally and celebrate continuously who God created you to become in Jesus' name. My sisters, I encourage you to think on these things and make them a habit!
